'MEET ME AT HAROLD WILSON'

Stories from St George's Square

Compiled by Christine Verguson and Beverley Norris
for Huddersfield Local History Society

Words and archive research: Christine Verguson

Images edited by Stephen Challenger

Huddersfield
Local
History
Society

Published by Huddersfield Local History Society
2023

© Copyright Huddersfield Local History Society

ISBN 978-0-9929841-6-8

Designed & Printed by Riasca

FRONT COVER CREDITS

Top Left:	Band of Hope Whitsuntide demonstration c1912 photographed by Lewis Cousens, courtesy Christopher R. Marsden.
Top centre:	'Hands Off HRI' rally, 23 January 2016, courtesy John Lambe.
Top right:	Garden with Venetian fountain, Kirklees Local Studies Library.
Middle left:	HERD Finale, courtesy Christopher R. Marsden.
Middle centre/right:	Courtesy Christine Verguson
Bottom left:	5th Battalion, West Riding Regiment, the Dukes, arriving at the station, 5 September 1914.
Bottom middle:	French Market 2014, courtesy John Lambe.
Bottom right:	Postcard, courtesy Christine Verguson

BACK COVER CREDIT

Festival of Light 2007, courtesy Alan Stopher.

Huddersfield Local History Society

'Meet you at the Harold Wilson statue!'

A mass cycle protest to New Mill

An organised Keep Britain Tidy community litter pick

A day out at the Food and Drink Festival.

An Xmas night out at the Hygge tent

Save Our A & E March (Huddersfield's biggest post-war march?)

An internet date with a guy from Lancashire

The global warning 'skip school' gathering

A walk up to Castle Hill with the Huddersfield Ramblers

A bank holiday Real Ale Trail expedition for a friend's 60th birthday

And the cherry on the cake, a local history society walk to explore the Square's development and beauty

KATIE, September 2021

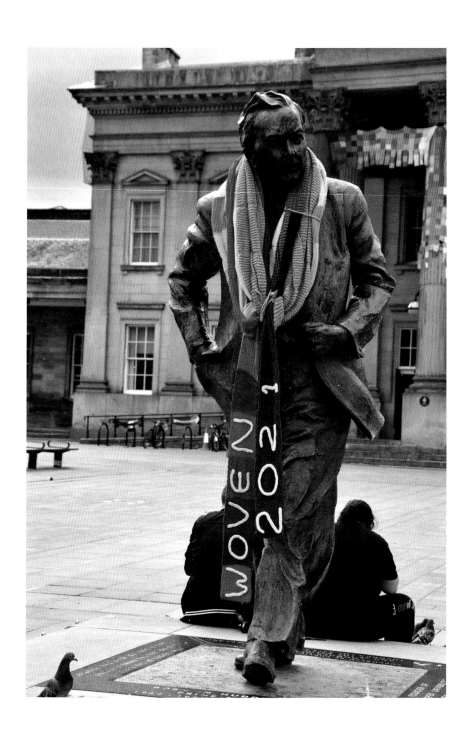

CONTENTS

FOREWORD

Huddersfield's High Streets Heritage Action Zone (HSHAZ), delivered in partnership with Kirklees Council, is part of a government-funded programme to unlock the potential of our high streets. We recognise the importance of our diverse communities in doing so and the contribution they give to making our historic areas so special. We wish to help people feel proud of where they live, work and visit. By collecting memories of people's visits to and interactions with St George's Square, the Memories of the Square project and this book will ensure that this and future generations will understand its cultural importance. We wish to thank Huddersfield Local History Society, Kirklees Council and all those who took the time to share their memories and research, resulting in this fantastic publication.

Charles Smith, Head of North Region, Historic England

Kirklees Council are pleased to be able to support this wonderful collection of memories and stories of St George's Square through the Huddersfield High Streets Heritage Action Zone (HSHAZ), in partnership with Historic England. The main aims of the Huddersfield HAZ are to repair and restore the George Hotel and the former Estates Building. However, it is not just our magnificent buildings around the Square but the story of our people, our rich and diverse communities which make Huddersfield so special. This fantastic book, partially funded through the HSHAZ, plays a crucial role in helping us tell our stories, our recollections of St George's Square and makes sure they can be told for many years to come. The Council congratulate Huddersfield Local History Society for bringing the book together and thank those who have contributed and Historic England for their funding contribution.

Nigel Hunston, Project Manager - Huddersfield High Streets Heritage
Action Zone, Kirklees Council

Three years ago when the Historic England grant to support community-led cultural activities here in Huddersfield was announced, Huddersfield Local History Society was chosen to take the lead in devising a history of St George's Square. At the time I expressed my pleasure that the Society was being honoured in this way and my excitement and hope that the project might lead us to a new approach to our local history.

With the creation of a dedicated website and now the publication of *Meet me at Harold Wilson*, I am proud to say that ambition has been realised. Discovering people's memories and blending them with more traditional historical research has created a real and innovative people's history of this much-loved part of the town.

Brian Haigh (1949-2021), the Local History Society's former Vice Chair, was an early member of the project's research team. His own deep understanding of the richness of the Square's history was an inspiration. Sadly, he died before the work was finished but his own feeling for the place has informed much of what is written here. As he wrote:

> *We all have different memories of the Square, of taking part in tapathons, watching Morris men or making the difficult choice of which world cuisine to taste. We may have negotiated our first mortgage at the Huddersfield (later Yorkshire) Building Society. We may have attended a company annual meeting or a wedding breakfast at the George or bought a gown from Madam Lucette's.*
>
> *All these activities, and many more, are woven into the collective memory which our project seeks to unravel and celebrate as its glorious buildings find new life and purpose.*

I confess that I never imagined that the Square had been the theatre in which so much of the last hundred and fifty years – and more - of Huddersfield's history had been played out or that it had been such an important part of so many people's lives and memories. For that I have to thank Brian, Beverley Norris, Christine Verguson and the rest of the project team who have written and compiled this splendid book - and, of course, the people of Huddersfield who have so freely shared their memories.

Cyril Pearce, Chair, Huddersfield Local History Society,
September 2023.

ACKNOWLEDGEMENTS

WE WOULD LIKE to thank all those people and organisations who have played a part in the making of this book:

Sylvia Arnold
Sally Barber
Katina Bill
David Blakeborough
Jo Blaker
Alan Brooke
Paul Brooks
Andrew Caveney
CHOL Theatre
Robert Clegg
Stephen Clegg
Val Davies
Annie Dearman
Ruth Dyer
Flaming Creations
Pat Fulgoni
Rebecca Gill
David Griffiths
Rosie Hall
Carol Hardy
Mark Hemingway
Tracie Hemphill
Jessica Herrett

Lee Hong Hirst
Richard Hobson
Jane Horton
Huddersfield Exposed
Huddersfield Hub
Huddersfield Photo-Imaging
    Club
Huddersfield St Patrick's
    Day Parade
Huddersfield Thespians
Huddersfield Town AFC
Huddersfield Urban
    Sketch Meets
Bill Jagger
Michelle Kain
Sharon Kelly
Roger Kinder
Kirklees Image Archive
Kirklees Local Studies
    Library
Kirklees Local TV
Knitting and Crochet Guild
John Lambe

Laura Lambe
Andy Lang
Steph Lawton
Adrian Lee
Let's Go Yorkshire
Chris Marsden
Janette Martin
Laura Mateescu
Jeff Mellor
Jenny Noake
Dave Pattern
Cyril Pearce
Alison Revell
Hilary Redfern
Dan Reilly
Helen Robinson
John Rumsby
Stan Sagan
Mandeep Samra
Grant Scanlan
Martin Shaw
Barry Sheerman MP
John Sheppard

Barbara Smith
Ian Stephenson
Oenone Stoodley
Alan Stopher
Catriona Swindells
Graham Sykes
Nick Tozer
Transpennine Express
David Verguson
Natalie Walton
Tosh Warwick
Kate Washburn
West Yorkshire Archive
    Service, Kirklees
White Rose Morris
Francis Wilson
David Wimpenny
Jeanette Wittford
Gordon Wood
Tim Worsnop
WOVEN in Kirklees
David Wyles

Every effort has been made to credit material included here where appropriate. We apologise in advance for any unintentional omission which we would be pleased to correct in any subsequent edition.

INTRODUCTION

THIS BOOK SETS out to explore how Huddersfield people, past and present, have experienced St George's Square. We all have our different memories of the Square. So many things have taken place here – happy and sad, public and personal. From the many businesses carried on in its splendid buildings to royal visits, carnivals, pageants, fairs and festivals of light, the Square has had a rich and colourful history. Politics, religion and sport have also played their part and, of course, the Rugby League was founded at the George Hotel. But there would be no Square without the railway station which has always been a place for arrivals and departures as well as for those just passing through.

Here we bring together living memories with eye-witness accounts from the past as well as maps and other snippets from the archives which relate to St George's Square. Some of the material included here has already appeared in a dedicated website, *Memories of Our Square* which, like this book, is part of Huddersfield Local History Society's contribution to Historic England's Huddersfield High Streets Heritage Action Zone (HS-HAZ) initiative. When we embarked on this project in 2020, we initially invited people to share their stories – in words or images – on our website. We also asked people at local history and archives-related events what the Square has meant to them. And in the summer of 2022, as part of our celebration of the Square and our mission to tell its story, we ran a photography competition asking for images captured since the beginning of 2020.

Mindful of the way content would be added to the website and our intention that the resulting book would not be an authored, chronological account, we saw the need to provide a Timeline listing significant events in the Square's history. Although added to subsequently, our Timeline (see pp.148-153) was created by the late Brian Haigh, local historian and Vice-Chair of our Society. Brian died in August 2021 but his contribution to this project has been immeasurable.

While a thematic approach has allowed us to reflect on the different types of activities and events that have taken place in St George's Square, it did

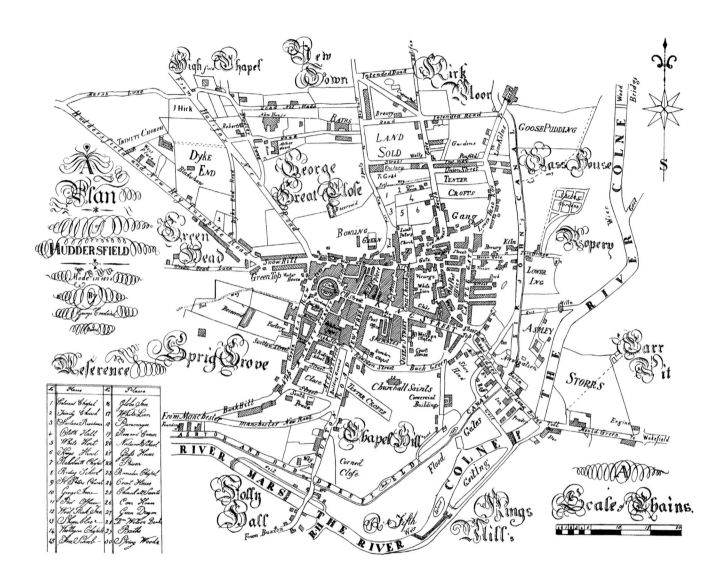

not seem to be the best way to explain how the town centre's biggest public space came into being and took the shape that it did. Instead, we have used two authored essays. Brian's account of the 'making of the Square' appears here with additional material from David Griffiths, who draws upon his extensive research on the Huddersfield Improvement Commissioners and the role played by the Ramsden family as Lords of the Manor. Although touching on some of the same material as Brian and David's article, David Wyles's essay, which was originally written for the website, looks at the beginnings of the Square from a different perspective, focusing on the buildings and their architects. We have also included a brief history of the George Hotel written by Brian Haigh.

Before the Square: George Crosland's map of Huddersfield, 1826, shows 'George Great Close', top left, where the station and Square would be built.

And while these essays celebrate St George's Square as a glorious addition to our town, we go on to show that almost from its beginning concerns, if not complaints, were being made about the Square's safety and appearance. Its architecture was also not without its critics and fountains, statues, flower beds and even bus stops have come and gone. Here, as in later sections of the book, observations from the past are augmented by living memories. We consider how the railway station has changed over the years and the experiences of some of those for whom it has been a point of arrival, with the Square providing their very first view of Huddersfield before they went on to make a life here for themselves. And, of course, the station is also a place from which people have departed for so many different reasons including a daily commute to work or setting off on their annual holidays.

While the textile magnates' warehouses that were so characteristic of St George's Square in the 19th century have now gone, it is still a place where business is carried out. And, starting with the George (at the time of writing being renovated so it can once again be used as a hotel) it has always been a place to socialise and find hospitality, although the types of shopping found here have changed over the years, and will change again. But both the station and the Square also provided opportunities for criminal activity which, thanks to reports from the Police Court, are well documented. Betting, in many different forms, was a particular problem. In addition, from firework incidents to royal visits, the police were responsible for maintaining order in the Square.

Much of the ongoing story of St George's Square is a consequence of its size and its ability to accommodate large numbers of people. Even before the main buildings had been completed, it provided a space for open-air election meetings, and the political rallies and protests held there would fill a book on their own. From suffragettes to conscientious objectors, together with the Market Place, it has provided a 'speaker's corner' for the people of Huddersfield. But while the Square has been a place for protesting, it has also been a place for patriotism to be displayed and victories celebrated. Royalty have been welcomed here, and some of the largest crowds to assemble in the Square have done so in the name of religion, particularly, but certainly not confined to, the annual parades around Whitsuntide. Sporting and musical events continue to play their part in the Square's story. From the beginning, the Square has served as a transport hub, but this has meant it has also been the scene for a number of accidents. In recent years the Square has played host to many popular fairs and festivals and animals have also played their part in the history of the Square. While putting this book together, it has also become clear that many of our stories relate to more than one of its themes.

Over the years St George's Square has inspired photographers, artists, and writers. There have also been many happenings in and around the Square resulting from the HS-HAZ initiative and this is reflected in the final section of this volume.

Meet Me at Harold Wilson does not set out to be a definitive history; it is, of necessity a selection, both on our part of what we have chosen to include from archival sources and on the part of those who have been generous enough to share some of their memories with us. We do not set out to provide a pictorial history of St George's Square – several good collections of old Huddersfield photos have already been published – but we have included many images because they are part of our story. We could not have done this without our colleagues at Kirklees Libraries and the Kirklees Image Archive as well as many others whose invaluable help is acknowledged elsewhere in this volume. Throughout the project we have been working with the West Yorkshire Archive Service who have not only given us access to the amazing documents in their collections which relate to St George's Square but have also undertaken to preserve the material we have collected for future generations. History will continue to be made in St George's Square.

A NOTE FOR READERS
As far as has been practical, the original spelling and grammar is used in quotes transcribed from archival sources.

THE MAKING
OF THE SQUARE

LAYING THE FOUNDATION STONE
OF THE HUDDERSFIELD STATION

...The whole of the members of the procession having been safely landed in the deep excavation prepared for them, Mr Pritchett, the Architect, handed over the trowel to Earl Fitzwilliam and preparations were at once made to lay the stone.

The foundation stone forms the corner stone of the front principal entrance, and was elevated a considerable height to enable Earl Fitzwilliam to spread the mortar, and deposit in a cavity beneath a bottle, containing the local newspapers of Saturday last, other documents and several coins. A brass plate was also deposited in the same cavity bearing the following inscription:-

"This Foundation-stone of the Huddersfield Station
of the Huddersfield and Manchester Railway
and Canal Company, built under the direction of the Board of
Directors, was laid by
THE RIGHT HON. THE EARL FITZWILLIAM,
This 9th day of October. A.D. 1846, being the
10th Year of her Majesty
Queen Victoria.
J. P. Pritchett and Co, Architects.
Joseph Kaye, Builder..."

Morning Herald, 14 October 1846

WHEN EARL FITZWILLIAM laid the foundation stone of Huddersfield Station in 1846 there were no plans to create a Square. But this was soon to change, as local historians relate in this chapter.

THE SQUARE THAT NEARLY WASN'T – A 'BREATHING SPACE' FOR THE TOWN

BRIAN HAIGH AND DAVID GRIFFITHS

IN THE EARLY 19th century, the line of Westgate and Kirkgate was pretty much the northern edge of built-up Huddersfield. Along Westgate in the 1820s were numerous shops and workshops and no fewer than seven pubs, and behind those, where Estate Buildings and Byram Arcade now stand, was a fast-growing jumble of commercial premises around yards. Beyond that, however, was open land – a bowling green across today's John William St, some adjoining gardens, and a large open field. Apparently named Great George Close, this was also known as 'Mr Wigney's tumbling field': Thomas Wigney was landlord of the old George Inn, in the Market Place, and a marquee on his field hosted itinerant entertainers. As the *Leeds Times* reported (27 May 1843) when the American animal trainer Isaac Van Amburgh visited the town: 'This gentleman will make his public entry into Huddersfield, next Saturday, June 3. The same day and on Monday the 5th, he will exhibit his wonderful performances with his trained lions and other wild animals, in a Marquee, in Mr. Wigney's field, Bradley Spouts.'

It was on this expanse of open ground that the Railway Station was built from 1846 to 1850. Initially reluctant to provide land for the railway, the Ramsden estate (the town's major landowner) had a change of heart when the railway companies agreed to purchase the Sir John Ramsden Canal and to compensate the family for any loss of income. From 1844 the estate's trustees, led by Earl Fitzwilliam of Wentworth Woodhouse and guided by

J. P. Pritchett's design for the railway station.

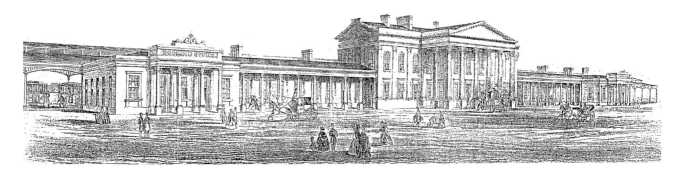

their new agent George Loch, supported plans to build a through line from Leeds to Manchester, in place of an earlier scheme limiting Huddersfield to a cul-de-sac branch to the town from Cooper Bridge. By 1850 there would be a line south to Barnsley and Sheffield too.

With the prospect of increased trade which the railways would bring, Loch set out plans to develop the open land around the Station. Initially there was no suggestion of a public square. Instead the land was laid out in lots to be leased for commercial development. These proposals called for the extension of New Street from the Market Place to form a new thoroughfare, John William Street, leading to the railway station and on to Bay Hall, where the estate had purchased land it also wanted to develop. (One early version of the plans also included a Ramsden Circus.) Named after Sir John William Ramsden, the fifth baronet (who would come of age in 1852), this required the demolition of the George, to be replaced by a grander hotel near the station. Built by Joseph Kaye, with stone remaining on site from the building of the station, the new George was completed in 1850 at a cost of £10,374 10s 7d. To ensure its success, the railway companies were not allowed to develop a hotel within the station, which explains why the 'stately home with trains in it', as it was described by architectural critic Ian Nairn in 1975, is not much more than a grand façade. The proposed developments would have hidden the elegant railway station. But the estate's agent Alexander Hathorn, Loch's full-time local deputy, writing to his boss, saw an opportunity to do better:

ALEXANDER HATHORN
to GEORGE LOCH

As you may not have the plan of this land with you, I enclose one on which I have marked the plot immediately in front of the New George, as to be left unlet, until the other principal lots have been disposed of, in the event of its being required for any Public Building. In considering the whole question, maturely, it has occurred to me, that seeing there is every possible prospect of all the rest of this land being let speedily and advantageously it might well be that this plot of land, in place of being built on at all, should be thrown open and formed into a Square – the whole effect would be very good, and would show our beautiful Railway Station and still more handsome (of its style) New George Hotel to infinite advantage.

West Yorkshire Archive Service (WYAS) Kirklees,
Ramsden Estate papers, DD/R/C/63, 27 August 1849

The Ramsden estate, however, was not the only player. Although Huddersfield Corporation lay 20 years in the future, a new body of largely-elected Improvement Commissioners had been established in 1848 with a range of local government powers. Their clerk, Joshua Hobson – also a political activist and eloquent journalist – took up the case in a series of articles published in the *Leeds Mercury* in December 1849 (the town's own first paper, the *Huddersfield Chronicle*, was launched in April 1850):

> ...In the first place, then, this plan is greatly deficient, in that it provides no open space, or square, to serve as lungs, or breathing space, for the inhabitants of the enlarged town. It is proposed to cover every portion of the available ground with buildings; making no provision even for increased market accommodation, for the increased and rapidly increasing inhabitants...
>
> In the next place the plan proposes to build up – to hide effectually from view – the elegant railway station erected by the public spirited directors of the Huddersfield and Manchester Railway...The building is a magnificent one – a great ornament to the town. And yet, in this plan of the new town, it is proposed so effectively to block it out with other buildings, as to leave only sixteen yards at the front open to view!..
>
> Joshua Hobson, *Leeds Mercury*, 15 December 1849

Portrait of Joshua Hobson (1810-1876) by Richard Waller, 1874, courtesy Kirklees Museums & Galleries.

In April 1850, following Hobson's lead, the Improvement Commissioners published their own plan. Drawn up by their surveyor, James Armytage, their version of the 'Square' was more of a triangle, but was linked to a generously extended Market Place flanked to its right by a new Town Hall, and with a large floral feature in the 'Square'. The old yards behind Westgate, which remained for decades longer, would have been swept away.

Events then moved quickly. The Commissioners approved their plan on 1 April and on the 5th appointed a deputation to present it to the estate. Hathorn described it to Loch on the 13th as an 'absurd affair, impracticable and utopian'; Loch consulted Lady Isabella; and she approved Hathorn's plan on the 18th.

The Square we have today is therefore more like the Ramsden plan than the Commissioners' one, but in the plan (overleaf) an added empty plot, where Britannia Buildings now stands, was slated for development. In this space, picking up an idea from Hobson, Loch proposed a town hall. This proposal had a tangled history but never came to pass.

At that time, a medley of public bodies had a hand in the governance of the town – the Improvement Commissioners (HIC) themselves, but also Waterworks Commissioners, Poor Law Guardians and Justices of the Peace. They met in various premises scattered around the town, often the George or other inns, and rarely purpose-built. A ratepayers' meeting back in 1843 had called for suitable rooms to be provided to accommodate meetings 'for every department of the Town's business' and to house all its civic documents. Hence the Improvement Commissioners' proposal for the Market Place site.

James Armytage's plan for the Improvement Commissioners, 1850, courtesy WYAS Kirklees.

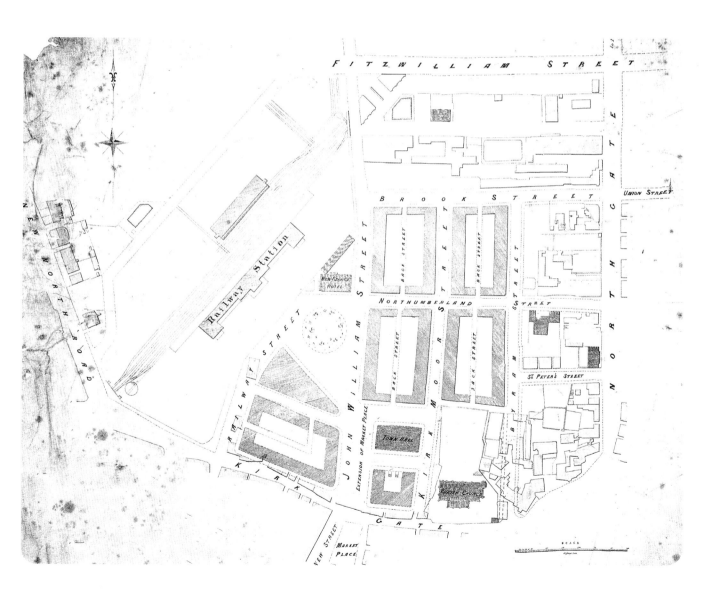

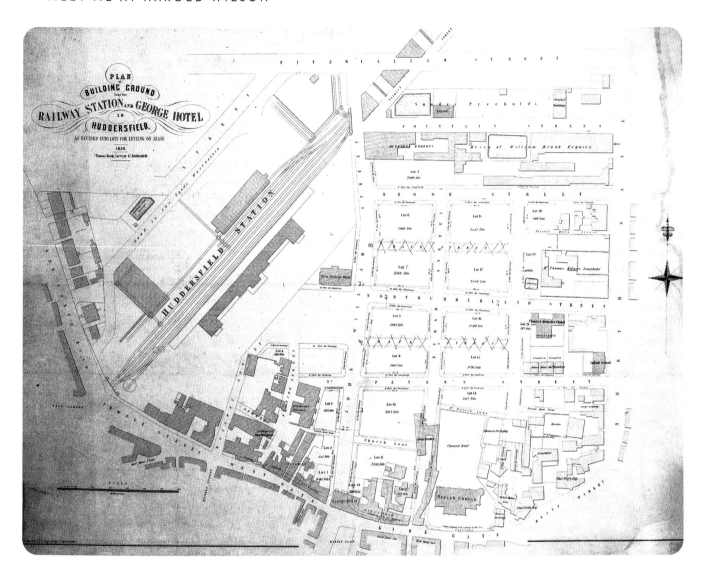

Plan of building ground near the railway station and George Hotel, Surveyor Thomas Brook, 1850, courtesy WYAS Kirklees.

This idea interested Hathorn and Loch, who saw that it would be in the estate's interest to have a prestigious building with reliable tenants on a vacant site opposite their new George Hotel, and they sounded out Sir John – not yet in charge, at 19 years old, but taking a growing interest in his inheritance. As reported by Loch, the young baronet 'expressed a perfect willingness to go into it' and indeed wished 'quietly and as a matter of course to take the entire lead, so far as the design and arrangements of the building are concerned'; Hathorn was to inquire what was needed, but was to be 'very careful not to say anything that will commit Sir John to any pecuniary contribution'. Working with Hobson, Hathorn moved quickly to collate the various bodies' requirements, now including the Post Office, adding his own suggestion for public halls and a dining room, with a tunnel to the George! The consultation was complete, and the results with Loch, by early December.

At which point the project stalled: all went quiet until August 1853 when the idea was revived by the newly established Chamber of Commerce and a joint Chamber/HIC committee was set up. They re-engaged with Hathorn; he approached Thomas Nelson, a London solicitor who had just replaced Loch as chief agent; and a very cool response was received. Faced with seeming lack of interest from Ramsden, the joint committee nonetheless commissioned a 'suggestive design' from Charles Pritchett, whose father James Pigott Pritchett had designed the station. Pritchett junior produced drawings for a domed classical building which would certainly have been an adornment to the Square and these were submitted to the Ramsden estate, but no agreement was reached between the various parties, and the town waited 25 years for a Town Hall.

The site on the South side of the Square remained empty until 1858, when woollen merchant George Crosland leased the plot and employed William Cocking to design a warehouse and office building. Britannia Buildings completed the square. Joshua Hobson, by that time editor of the *Huddersfield Chronicle*, was delighted with the results, which created what he described as 'one of the finest vistas in the provinces' and which has provided the magnificent legacy we still celebrate today.

Charles Pritchett's 'suggestive design' for a town hall in the Square (never built), courtesy WYAS Kirklees.

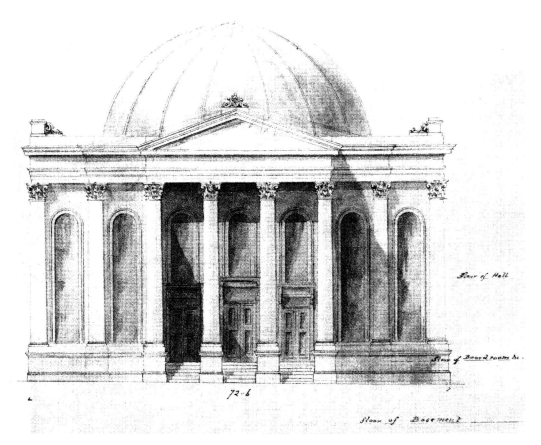

BUILDING THE SQUARE – THE POWER AND THE GLORY

DAVID WYLES

THOSE STEPPING OUT of the station into St. George's Square for the first time cannot fail to be impressed by the quality of the grand Victorian buildings that face them. For not only does St. George's Square contain one of the finest collections of architecturally and historically important buildings in the north of England but it contains perhaps the finest of all railway stations in the UK, described by the architectural critic, Ian Nairn, as 'a kind of stately home with trains in'.

Born of the ambitions of the Lords of the Manor of Huddersfield, the Ramsden family, and driven by the rapid commercial growth of the town, the area around the Square, known as the 'new town', can be likened to the rapid growth and ascendency of Italy's great maritime powers during the Renaissance. In fact, it is to these cities and to their forebears, from Classical Greece and Rome, that we can follow a story of commercial acumen, increasing wealth and a desire to impress.

These are not buildings that evoke delight in the way that, say, those former woollen towns of the Cotswolds cast their charm. These are robust and formal, sturdy and dignified, transmitting a sense of wealth and power. They are refined and balanced in proportion and mass, the exception being the Ramsden Estate Office, built between 1870-74, over fifteen years after most other buildings around the Square had been completed, which is an exceptional interpretation of High Victorian Gothic. Their sense of permanence is reinforced with the use of local York sandstone, ideally suited for sawing and tooling and able to withstand those years of industrial pollution. This is a location where the skill of the architect is matched by the skills of those masons who dressed and sculpted the raw material.

These buildings were built to impress but look behind their facades and what becomes apparent is that these palaces of power were used primarily as offices and warehousing for the burgeoning textile industry that established the town's reputation worldwide for the quality of its cloth.

And yet, the grandeur of these buildings is partly undermined by the open space which constitutes the Square. For this is not a square in the conventional sense. It is a space that seeps away in several directions with the effect that the physical grouping of buildings is dispersed across a wide, less than formal area. The grid of the 'new town' is not apparent at this point and, it could be argued, the harmony of the whole does not match the quality of the individual buildings.

Although the Ramsden family had promoted the town as a commercial hub with the building of the Cloth Hall (1766) and Sir John Ramsden Canal (1774-80), the latter extended by the Huddersfield Narrow Canal across (and under) the Pennines, the town remained relatively cramped and poorly planned. The canals had allowed goods in far greater quantity to be exported across the country and via the ports of Liverpool and Hull but Huddersfield's greatest disadvantage by the 1840s was the lack of a direct link by train. The idea of a line from Huddersfield had been proposed in 1835 but many years of bitter argument passed between the Trustees of the Ramsden Estate, the townspeople and speculators, before an Act of Parliament in 1845 authorised the building of the line.

An open site was selected for the new station on the east side of the town, and work on levelling the ground commenced in December 1845. The architect was J.P. Pritchett (1789-1868) who also designed the Parish Church of St. Peter and the Huddersfield College on New North Road.

The builder was Joseph Kaye (1780-1858) who was responsible for building many of the finest buildings in the town including Holy Trinity (1816-19), Queen Street Chapel (1819), Ramsden Street Chapel (1824), St. Paul's (1829), the Infirmary (1829-31), St. Patrick's (1832), St. John's, Birkby (1852) and the George Hotel. He was probably responsible for many of the other buildings in the 'new town'.

There are several factors, which led to the creation of what we see today. Firstly, the controlling influence of the Ramsden family, at the time under control of trustees, with Isabella Ramsden acting as guardian to the young John William, the fifth baronet, and whose brother-in-law, Earl Fitzwilliam, was one of the country's most prominent politicians and landowners; his influence on the development of the Square was certainly key to its creation. They appointed an astute auditor and land agent, George Loch, to manage the estate. Loch negotiated the beneficial location of the station and the purchase of surrounding land, on behalf of the Ramsdens. Loch realised the potential value of the land in front of the station, but it was inaccessible because the existing George Inn, standing across the end of New Street prevented satisfactory access. In January 1849 Loch suggested the demolition of the inn, the building of a new hotel and the extension of the main street to provide 'a proper approach to the station'. Within a few days Isabella Ramsden had approved Loch's proposals as well as his idea that the new street be named after her son.

The efforts of the local activist and journalist, Joshua Hobson, whose articles in the *Leeds Mercury* criticised Loch's proposals to crowd as many properties as possible into the area around the station, were taken up by the newly created Improvement Commissioners for the town by whom

Portrait of Joseph Kaye (1780-1858), unknown artist, courtesy Kirklees Museums and Galleries.

Hobson, by that time, was employed as Clerk of Works. The Commissioners' proposals were accepted by the Trustees who, by December 1850, agreed 'to leave nearly the whole of the elegant station front open to view from the very centre of town, forming one of the finest architectural vistas in the provinces'.

The next key element to the Square's appearance lies in the architects who were commissioned to oversee the development and design the buildings. J.P. Pritchett secured the commission for the station, having previously worked for Earl Fitzwilliam. His designs, based on classical Greek architecture, were equally influenced by Fitzwilliam's stately home at Wentworth Woodhouse, with its impressive portico and Corinthian columns. By the time the station was completed in 1850 the Greek Revival had become passé but Classical influences prevailed. The George Hotel by local architect William Wallen was the first building to be completed in 1850 and established a benchmark for further development in the Italianate style.

In 1851 William Tite was appointed to oversee the design of individual buildings as they were submitted for approval by the Ramsden Trustees. Tite was already a well-established and prosperous architect who favoured classical design and most of the buildings reflect his taste for the palazzi built by wealthy families during the Italian Renaissance. Pritchett, who by the early 1850s had fallen out of favour with the Ramsdens, designed Lion Buildings for Samuel Oldfield, though Tite rejected initial proposals, later informing George Loch that 'they are greatly indebted to me for putting a very crude design into shape and proportion'.

Arguably, the grandest building is Britannia Buildings (1856-59), designed by William Cocking for merchant manufacturer George Crosland and Sons, with its full-blooded interpretation of the palazzo, incorporating boldly sculpted masks, rustication, scrolled brackets and rich festoons with its central parapet bearing the Royal Arms above which is the sculpted figure of Britannia.

It was the Estate Buildings that broke the mould, with a design by Huddersfield born W. H. Crossland, who had established his reputation with his designs for Rochdale Town Hall and was to develop a distinctive interpretation of Gothic architecture that culminated in his outstanding design for the Royal Holloway College in Surrey. The Estate Office was a clear break from the Classical traditions that had predominated and followed a period when the 'Battle of Styles' was fiercely contested between the supporters of the Gothic and the Classical. The architectural and decorative flamboyance of Crossland's scheme is striking, incorporating intricate sculptural details, the use of wrought iron and granite as well as introducing turrets, trefoil-headed windows and many other features that successfully add charm but retain the overall grandeur of the architecture of the Square.

Perhaps the final factor in the story of the Square is the least documented. Much has been written over the past 40 years about the Ramsdens, their

The Stonemason's art, Estate Buildings, courtesy Christine Verguson.

Britannia on top of her building, courtesy Stephen Challenger.

Estate Buildings montage, courtesy Graham Sykes, Huddersfield Photo-Imaging Club.

agents and architects but little is known about the masons who cut and tooled the sandstone and sculpted the decorative features. Draw close to these buildings to admire and even touch the stonework, noting the copings, cornices and balustrades, armorials, tracery, balustrades, festoons, ornate capitals and, especially on the Estate Office, the elaborate carvings of birds, animals, flowers and foliage and, for those with sharp eyes, the bare bottom of a naked man. The power and the charm of these buildings lies as much in these features, some of which were said to have been carved in situ, and perhaps further research will cast a light on the toil and skills of these unnamed people.

FROM NAIRN'S JOURNEY: FOOTBALL TOWNS 2: HUDDERSFIELD AND HALIFAX

It is more of a palace than a station, a kind of stately home with trains in … Now the Corporation owns the station building, the station yard and part of platform one. Thank God they did, because it could so easily have gone the way of Euston Arch, and all around here, at the end of the 1840s, was built a really solid, grand Victorian square complete with fountain. A grand introduction to the town, but alas, that is almost all there is.

First transmitted on BBC ONE, 21 August 1975

THE STATE OF
THE SQUARE

AS FAR AS celebrated architectural critic and broadcaster Ian Nairn (1930-1983) was concerned, when it came to Huddersfield v. Halifax, despite his praise for St George's Square, the station and it seems little else, Halifax won the game! But this was not the only thing Nairn didn't get right - the Square was not 'complete with fountain' until the 1970s. And even in the 1850s when the Square was new, not everyone was happy with the way it looked. In January 1858 'E.R.' wrote to the Editor of the *Huddersfield Chronicle* on the subject of the 'town's architectural and decorative taste' and while he found much to admire, there were also 'many instances' which showed 'a sad want of taste' and this was particularly true of St George's Square.

> ...I cannot help grieving to see so lamentable a mismanagement of one of the finest sites in Yorkshire. There was every advantage;- you had first-rate stone and materials, plenty of space, endless wealth; and then to find such splendid buildings thrown into an unshapely, awkward-looking, falsely-called Square! Sir, I may be charged with affected feelings of architectural fastidiousness; but I cannot help thinking and saying, that, with such palace-like warehouses on one side, the railway station on another, the George Hotel on the third, every stranger who alights from the railway must be filled with amazement that so much money could have been expended and so ineffective a result attained.
>
> E. R. *Huddersfield Chronicle*, 23 January 1858

On 17 September 1859 Ambler Woodhead, an ostler at Huddersfield's Imperial Hotel, was on his way to the railway station to collect a guest when he had to turn 'suddenly' into St George's Square to avoid 'an old man' and was thrown out of his dogcart, fracturing his skull. At the inquest into his death cab owner Thomas Cooper, who had witnessed the accident, told the jury that Woodhead 'turned rather sharply round his cab, and on going off the street sets onto the square, the drop caused him to leave his seat'. The jury foreman remarked that he had seen many narrow escapes there and that the drop should be referred to Sir John W. Ramsden who owned the Square. The jury were quick to return a verdict of accidental death but added that Ambler Woodhead's fall had been partly caused by the 'unfinished state of St George's Square' (*Huddersfield Chronicle*, 24 September 1859).

Outside Britannia Buildings before the Square was paved, courtesy Kirklees Local Studies Library.

Over the years there have been many comments on the state and, indeed, safety of the Square, with some correspondents even offering their own suggestions.

ST GEORGE'S-SQUARE. – A SUGGESTION

SIR, - Knowing that your columns are always open to the public when the interests of Huddersfield are involved, would you allow me as a visitor to call public attention to the very disgraceful state of St. George's-square? Why that locale was dubbed with this high and exalted name I cannot guess...

During ten years past I have frequently had occasion to visit Huddersfield, and I have always been impressed with the constant progress of improvements. But the moment I get to the Railway Station steps my progress is delayed. I am then driven to think and plan how I can best wade across the Square.

As a stranger I cannot imagine why a spot of such importance is left in such a disgraceful and dangerous condition as it is, and no one seems to take any interest in setting matters right, perhaps you could allow me to suggest a mode of raising sufficient funds to enable the owner or owners (if there be such) to put this fine open space into tolerable repair.

...I propose that a penny contribution be set on foot and that collecting boxes be placed at each corner of the Square for its receipt. For my own part I feel that the charitable disposition of the Huddersfield public is such that if it is only appealed to upon this matter before long this Square will cease to be the civic reproach that it is...

PROGRESS (London), *Huddersfield Chronicle*, 28 January 1871

Although the suggestion to provide collection boxes was never acted on, improvements were being made to the Square. In April 1870 the Ramsden estate had offered the area of the Square to Huddersfield Corporation provided they laid down paving and an order was made in the Huddersfield Improvement Act of 1871 for the long over-due paving of the Square. In the same month a meeting of the Borough Council agreed that this would be completed by the first day of February 1872.

Moving the motion, Councillor Jordan's remark that 'he had not had a more pleasing duty for some time' and that 'there was not a place in the town that required [repairs] more than the square' was greeted with applause. Alderman Brooke, chairing the meeting described a 'humorous scene' he had witnessed when, a 'commercial', in crossing the Square, had 'lost his boots'! The paving work had still not been started when a letter from 'A

Large Ratepayer' appeared in the *Huddersfield Chronicle* on 24 February 1872, urging the Corporation not to simply 'pave the Square with sets as they would a town's yard' but to follow plans that had been put before them which would result in the adornment of the Square, even if this would delay things: 'The site is too large and imposing in every way to be dealt with as though it were a mere yard. No town in England possesses a finer opening on leaving the railway station and I hope the good taste of those who have the power will be brought into exercise to avert its being sacrificed'.

As the Square took shape in the 1850s, it is clear that the Ramsdens did think it needed some sort of centrepiece, but no design then met with their approval. A drinking fountain for the Square was considered and a water-colour sketch has survived. There was some discussion of heraldry associated with the Ramsden family and Isaac Hordern, whose 'suggestive' design was worked up by W. H. Crossland, called it the 'Armorial Fountain'. In January 1950 a prize was awarded to W. T. Boyd from the Borough Architect's Department for his design for an ornamental stone fountain and floral surround which was intended to form a central island in the Square. But according to local historian Stanley Chadwick the plan for a fountain was vetoed by the government. When the Square did finally get its fountain it was second-hand; the Venetian fountain which came to Huddersfield from a

Isaac Hordern's design for a proposed Armorial fountain, 1860, courtesy WYAS Kirklees.

"It is resolved and ordered by the Council of the borough of Huddersfield that the following street, namely, St. George's-square, being a street within the borough, and not being a highway usually repaired by the inhabitants at large, be freed from obstruction, sewered, drained, levelled, flagged, paved, kerbed, and otherwise completed at such levels, and with such inclinations, and with sewers and drains, and that the soil thereof be raised, lowered or altered in such manner as are, or is respectively shown on the plan, drawing, and section thereof deposited in the office of the Borough surveyor..."

Huddersfield Chronicle,
23 December 1871

Borough Architect Derek Vane's sketch "Proposed fountain", courtesy Oenone Stoodley.

London dealer's yard was over 100 years old. Its basin was 20 feet in diameter and, as with the 1950 plan, was intended as a centrepiece for a floral island. It was switched on by the last Mayor of the County Borough of Huddersfield, Councillor John Mernagh, on 26 March 1974 and the departing Council was commemorated by an inscription. The fountain featured three seahorses, two bowls and a boy with a fish as well as lighting which could only be seen at night. Take a look at Borough Architect Derek Vane's sketch of the 'proposed fountain' and see if you can identify any of these features. There were those who thought that the Venetian fountain was an extravagance or that it looked out of place in the Square and its time was cut short due to erosion caused by acid rain.

I remember the lovely flowers on the roundabout and the fountain at St George's Square, the long row of bus stops and once feeding pigeons with my mum. You can't do that any more.

TRACIE HEMPHILL, September 2021

Although I liked the floral display in the Square, and the parked trolley buses between duties in the circle made for them, I think it's redesign to a more open pedestrian area was an improvement. I look forward to the newly restored buildings around this area.

JOHN SHEPPARD, September 2021

Children playing in fountains, courtesy Janette Martin.

By 1989 there was a new plan for the Square which eventually resulted in a very different water feature. The jet fountains accompanied by a granite water cascade at the bottom of the Square that we see today were first turned on in October 2009, a year behind schedule. Children could play in the water, but the flowers had gone.

Writing to the *Huddersfield Chronicle* in December 1886, Mr J. W. Scholes listed 17 suggestions which he thought could benefit the town. His was an ambitious list which included a free library and a public art gallery, but his final suggestion was for 'fountains and trees in St George's Square, with a statue of the Queen, in commemoration of the Jubilee' which was due to take place in 1887. Having 'flitted' through Bradford's Forster Square, the *Examiner*'s columnist 'Ariel' was impressed by its flower beds and walks.

An 'improvement plan' was announced for the Square in April 1937 which was mainly concerned with traffic flow resulting from the replacement

---

What a glorious thing, if our noble St George's Square, instead of being converted into a hideous, if useful, street railway terminus and coaling station, had been lain out in flower beds; and grass plots; of course making all due provision for access to and from the station and its approaches. Alas! It is too late for that now. But why not utilise the Old Market Place. – as I believe it was once proposed to do. The "world menders" and itinerant lecturers, the gossips and the street loafers, might find another place in which to air their stale platitudes and course wit.

'Ariel', Supplement, *Huddersfield Daily Examiner*, 18 June 1892

---

of the electric trams by trolley-buses but 'nearer to the market place there will be left parking space for a few "buses" and an island, which is to be laid out with grass and flower beds, will occupy the site of the present run of tram rails' (*Yorkshire Observer*, 13 April 1937). It may be that the garden part of the project was delayed by the Second World War. In March 1950 the *Huddersfield Daily Examiner* could refer to 'the tentative plan to improve St George's Square twenty years or so ago which left us with a couple of carefully prepared mud-heaps in the middle of it…'. In May the Borough's Parks and Cemeteries Committee reported that plans were in hand to plant the flowers in the gardens already laid out in the Square while the Borough Engineer recommended that flower baskets be attached to the trolley vehicle poles. In February 1953 the Corporation announced its plan for the decoration of the Square for Queen Elizabeth II's Coronation, where the garden would provide the centrepiece.

> The circular garden in the square will form the centrepiece of the decorative scheme. A flag pole is to be permanently erected in the middle of the garden to which will be built a decorated circular base. Four pennants are to be suspended from the pole itself and a crown will appear at the top. The flower beds are to be specially planted for the occasion.
>
> The trolley standards surrounding the square – which are already fitted with flower baskets – will be draped with pennants and bunting.
>
> *Yorkshire Post and Leeds Mercury*, 13 February 1953

The flagpole can be clearly seen in one of the images showing the garden in the Square in the early 1970s but in the second photo it has disappeared, probably to make room for the Venetian fountain.

Some time before the Second World War flowers were planted around the statue of Sir Robert Peel but by 1947 the *Yorkshire Observer* felt the need to ask, 'What will happen to Sir Robert?'. The iron railings surrounding the statues had been requisitioned as part of the war effort and the chair of the Highways Committee told the newspaper, 'The statue is now in rather a decrepit state.' The statue had been unveiled on 3 June 1873, 23 years after Peel's death. Efforts in Huddersfield to collect subscriptions (by two different committees!) started shortly after the death of the former Prime Minister but came to nothing. A new committee was formed in 1869 and a design

LEFT
*Garden with flagpole,
courtesy WYAS Kirklees.*

BELOW
*Garden without flagpole
also showing the Venetian
fountain, courtesy Kirklees
Local Studies Library.*

from sculptor William Theed the younger was accepted. A dispute with the Ramsden estate about the placing of the statue followed and it was eventually sited on land owned by the railway company in front of the station. Although funded by public subscription the Corporation paid the company an annual rent for the land.

DESCRIPTION OF THE STATUE

The statue, which in itself is nine feet high, is cut out of Sicilian marble, single block, and weighs three and a half tons...The robe is that worn by the Chancellor of the Exchequer, and has been carefully modelled from the one used by the present occupant of that high office, which was courteously lent for the purpose by Mr Lowe, and was adopted to mark the great financial reputation of Sir Robert, and at the same time to give more lofty and statuesque effect to that figure. In his left hand the deceased statesman holds a scroll, to which he is pointing with the right hand, in allusion probably to his successful labours in the repeal of the Corn Laws. Including the pedestal, the statue is 30 feet high. The pedestal has been executed by the celebrated firm of MacDonald and Field, of Aberdeen, in grey Aberdeen marble, and two or three Yorkshire-stone steps have been added by Mr Cocking, architect, Huddersfield, to increase its elevation. In front of the pedestal, there is a fine bronze relief of "Feeding the Hungry". Also from a design of Mr Theed, which is a very direct reference to the benefit conferred upon the working classes by the repeal of the Corn Laws. At the back of the statue is the following celebrated extract from the speech of Sir Robert Peel:- "It may be that I shall leave a name sometimes remembered with expressions of goodwill in the abodes of those whose lot it is to labour and to earn their bread by the sweat of their brow; when they shall recruit their exhausted strength with abundant and untaxed food, the sweeter because it is no longer leavened with a sense of injustice."

Huddersfield Chronicle, 4 June 1873

Not only was every aspect of the statue's unveiling by Lord Houghton chronicled in the local press but the scene showing the size of the crowd, not to mention the people on the station roof, was captured by the *Illustrated London News* which had already run an article with an engraving and description of Mr Theed's 'colossal statue'. But, having stood outside in the acid rain for 76 years, in 1949 the Peel statue was removed from the Square to a Council depot. It was decided that the statue was too dilapidated to be re-erected elsewhere but a home for its granite plinth was eventually found in Ravensknowle Park.

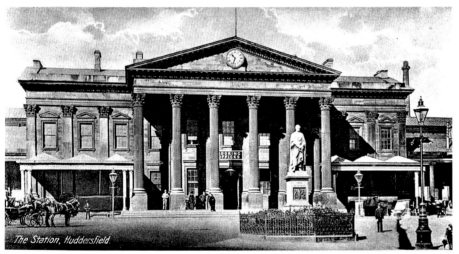

TOP LEFT
Lord Houghton unveiling the statue of Sir Robert Peel, from the Illustrated London News, *21 June 1873.*

LEFT
Postcard, Peel statue in place in front of the station, courtesy Christine Verguson.

ABOVE
Detailed sketch of the Huddersfield Peel Statue, Illustrated London News, *14 June 1873.*

Fifty years after one Prime Minister was taken out of the Square, another one took his place. Designed by Ian Walters, the bronze statue of Huddersfield-born Harold Wilson - 6ft 8ins in height and standing on a black marble kerb on a 4ft high plinth of Crosland Moor stone - was unveiled by Prime Minister Tony Blair on 9 July 1999. It seems to be the case that statues in the Square have been more warmly received by Huddersfield people than have fountains.

Take a close look at the pictures appearing throughout this book and see how the Square's lamps have changed over the years. As the *Electrical Engineer* reported on 1 December 1893: 'Huddersfield Saint George's Square is the first public thoroughfare in Huddersfield to be lighted by electricity.

The Harold Wilson statue. The one I voted for. The day of unveiling by current PM Tony Blair – he arrived by car at great speed down Westgate (why at speed?) – seen from my Westgate office. At lunchtime I popped down (again!) for a nosey. A very grand affair it had been with well laid out chairs and floral decorations (presumably from Kirklees before they got rid of the nurseries!) with the resplendent Harold in full view. I saw him in the flesh just once – 1974, Buxton Road, for what I cannot recall but it was when he refused to release the doves! My overriding memory is his piercing blue eyes. Not to be crossed! Back to the later PM, Tony Blair. It turned out he was in The George and was about to leave, which he did, again at speed. Perhaps he was being chased?!

ADRIAN LEE, March 2022

My mum absolutely loved the Harold Wilson statue. The son of Huddersfield, which made her very proud.

MICHELLE KAIN, October 2022

I attended the reception following the unveiling of the statue by then PM, Tony Blair and attended by Lady Wilson. Some expected to see Harold with a pipe in his hand or mouth, but, as Lady Wilson explained, the pipe was used mainly as a prop, to provide a pause when he was making a speech and a tool for helping emphasise a point. She had wanted the sculpture to be an informal representation, rather than a caricature with pipe and Gannex coat.

DAVID WYLES, December 2021

One of the memories I have in the Square that stands out is when we unveiled the statue of Harold Wilson at the centre. Harold had always been a great source of local information. He had been the one to tell me about the George Hotel's heritage as the birthplace of Rugby League — "the bosses didn't want to pay 'em". Many years later when it came time to erect a statue to Harold I organised for Tony Blair to be the one to come and unveil it. The Wilson family, Tony and I sat in the George Hotel enjoying a drink and talking about Harold and the town he'd loved, with the Square right at its heart.

BARRY SHEERMAN MP, February 2023

I too was there for the unveiling – with Lady Wilson taking part of course as well as Tony Blair. My abiding image is of a large throng around the Square, in memory's eye mainly female, and of ripples of comment about what a nice young man he seemed to be. He was still in his 'Bambi' phase, with the Iraq war and other troubles well in the future. The sun shone (I think!) and Britain might even have seemed to be the 'young country' of those early Blairite years.

DAVID GRIFFITHS, May 2023

27

The current was turned on for the first time on Wednesday. Three powerful arc lamps on high pillars are found ample for the illumination of the large square'. *The Huddersfield Chronicle* described where the lamps were situated, 'immediately opposite Sir Robert Peel's monument, and the others on each side of the square on the corners nearest the George Hotel and Britannia-buildings', adding that while the lighting provided by the large arc lamps was said to be a great improvement, the light provided was 'hardly as brilliant as most people expected it would be'.

Over the years the appearance of the bus shelters in the Square has been commented on. In 1951 the Huddersfield branch of the West Yorkshire Society of Architects wrote to the Mayor protesting about the erection of a bus shelter: 'The outcome cannot be regarded as anything but complete and total defilement of a vista which, from the juncture of Westgate with Railway Street, had a most pleasing and artistic appearance' (*Yorkshire Post*, 27 October 1951).

Mrs Emily Haigh, 76, had emigrated to the United States in 1905 but when she returned home for a visit in June 1950, she told the *Daily Examiner* that the town had 'altered since her last visit, and she has noticed many improvements – particularly in St George's Square.

I think the lamps were removed, the first time they altered the Square but they've altered it so many times. They are still round the Town Hall and in St Peter's Gardens. They were made out of aluminium but these things were only put there in 1985. They've only been up about ten years, It could have been 1980, but I remember the station without them and all those horrible concrete bus shelters by the Alassio restaurant. They ran from the corner of that building right down to nearly where the George Hotel is. They looked like something that had just been put up temporarily, just after the war maybe.

DAVID WIMPENNY, December 2022

My association with St George's Square goes back to 1962 when I went to school in Elland. We caught the West Vale bus from the Square with a sloping roof. I also remember the 'scarab' British Rail vehicles working in the Square.

PAUL BROOKS, May 2022

I think of St George's Square as a bit of an ugly place, it still is, but I've enjoyed the festivals, giants, big balloons and concerts that have taken place there... a good use of all that space! I don't mind the buses going round, it's a continuation of previous usage.

STAN SAGAN, March 2022

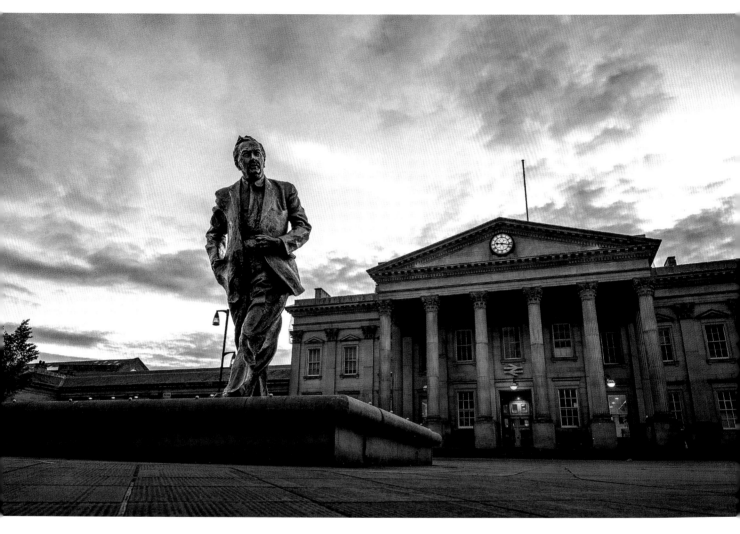

'Walking with a purpose' photographed by Francis Wilson – runner up in the Capturing St George's Square 2020-2022 photo competition.

The next application, of Mr William Padmore, for licensing the Railway Refreshment Rooms – four rooms, on the ground-floor, a smoking room, and waiting-room and two others up-stairs – was supported by Mr Freeman and strongly opposed to the extent applied for, by Mr Floyd. After some discussion – a licence was granted for the four rooms on the ground-floor, a smoking room and waiting room on the second storey.

Huddersfield Chronicle, 24 August 1850

LONDON AND NORTH WESTERN AND LANCASHIRE AND YORKSHIRE RAILWAY REFRESHMENT ROOMS, HUDDERSFIELD STATION,

THE DIRECTORS of these Companies are prepared to receive TENDERS for the LETTING of their REFRESHMENT ROOMS for such period as may be agreed upon, and will meet in the BOARD ROOM, at the HUDDERSFIELD STATION, on FRIDAY, the 13th SEPTEMBER to open Tenders for the same.
The Tenders must be endorsed "Tender for the Huddersfield Station Refreshment Rooms" and addressed to WILLIAM GILMER, Secretary to the Huddersfield and Manchester Local Committee, Huddersfield, 30th August 1850.

Huddersfield Chronicle, 7 September 1850

AT THE STATION

THE FIRST PEOPLE to live in the newly created Square were the station master William Padmore and his family. Padmore had been given the job of Huddersfield's first ever station master in 1847; the census shows that in 1851 he was living at the station with his wife Ann and their five children. The youngest child, Sarah, was only three weeks old at the time of the census so she may have even been born in the station. It was Padmore who applied to the Brewster Session to obtain a licence for the Railway Refreshment Rooms in 1850. Living alongside the Padmore family at the station were innkeeper George Moore, his wife Mary, stepson Charles, niece Sarah – described as a 'house servant' – and two further house servants, both called Mary.

As many Huddersfield people are aware, our station is unusual because, when it opened it was used by two different railway companies with their own booking offices on either side of the platform and whose company crests

RIGHT
The Lancashire and Yorkshire Railway Company's coat of arms.

FAR RIGHT
Huddersfield & Manchester Railway & Canal Company coat of arms, both courtesy Stephen Challenger.

can still be seen today. The booking office for the London and North Western Railway (LNWR) is now the King's Head, formerly the Station Tavern, while that used by the Lancashire and Yorkshire Railway (L&YR) is now the Head of Steam which opened in 1996. When Nick Tozer came to work in Huddersfield in the late 1980s, there were still traces of the 19th century booking office.

Originally the Station Refreshment Rooms occupied the centre of the building. While the Refreshment Rooms were often referred to as the Station Hotel, there is no evidence that the hotel was residential. Although the Moore family lived there with their staff and with the number of servants increasing over the years, no boarders were ever listed in the census returns.

The Refreshment Rooms provided food and drink for those passing through or arriving at the station although different 'classes' of travellers were catered for. When, in 1877, F.R.D of Bradford complained that, having gone into the First Class Refreshment Room, he could not have lunch before 1pm, he got short shrift from the *Chronicle's* editor who declared: 'Thousands of

HOTELS, WINE AND SPIRIT MERCHANTS

————————

STATION HOTEL, HUDDERSFIELD
(Under new management)
S. BAYLIS (late of the George Hotel)
begs to inform the residents and visitors of
Huddersfield that he has taken the above
hotel, and trusts that his past experience in
catering for the public will be a guarantee
for the future.
Table d'hôte from One till
Two, 2s6d per head.
Cold Collation, Teas, Coffee, &c.,
at all hours

Huddersfield Chronicle, 20 May 1882

Where the Head of Steam is now, was the Lancashire and Yorkshire's booking office and when I came up, behind there was a big old sill and doors that were rarely if ever opened that gave access to that end of the platform. The ticket windows were still there and actually the booking office. If you went in it was as if they'd walked out some years back, and it had just got dusty and rotten and horrible, and then as you went along you had the mess rooms for the train crew, guards and drivers but when the Head of Steam came they took over part of the mess room and all of that former 'Lanky' booking office.

NICK TOZER, former train driver, May 2023

Our grandfather (on our mother's side) used to take us into Huddersfield when we were little, in the late 1950s, and we often visited the railway station with our one-penny platform tickets. At that time the waiting room and the café had coal fires, and my sister remembers not one but TWO roaring fires in the café. We usually went in for a warming cup of Bovril, whist our grandad chatted with the lady behind the counter, standing with his back to the fire to keep himself warm.

SYLVIA ARNOLD & ALISON REVELL, December 2021

other travellers, similarly situated, have taken refuge in the same port, and found it one of the best in the provinces 'provided for the convenience of passengers'". The editor concluded that F.R.D. 'must be somewhat hard to please'.

In June 1882 the licence for the Station Hotel passed from George Moore's widow Esther to caterer Samuel Bayliss - the owner is listed as the LNWR – and in the following year the licence passed to Samuel's widow, Emily. Her son, Samuel, managed the hotel but the family did not move in. When in June 1891 a warehouse man was charged with breaking and entering the Station Hotel, Samuel Bayliss stated that he had locked up at 11.20pm. However, in 1911, in the latest census return we have been able to find for the Refreshment Rooms, ten women lived there, all described as 'spinsters'. In addition to manageress Alice Jones, four worked as 'bar assistants', two as waitresses and there was also a cook, a kitchen maid and a scullery maid. The two separate railway company booking offices had been replaced in 1886 by a joint booking office in the central part of the station. Were the Refreshment Room workers accommodated above the Booking Office? A British Rail plan from 1949 shows that the Refreshment Rooms were situated where the King's Head is today with the kitchen, scullery and keeping cellars below. Two hearths are shown in the main seating area. Sisters Sylvia Arnold and Alison Revell remember that when they were children, the station was a good place to go to get refreshments as well as to get warm.

Until recently the independently run 'old style station buffet' on Platform Four was popular with both commuters and railway workers. Narrowly avoiding closure in 2005 when Transpennine Express - who managed the station - wanted to provide a new waiting room, it finally shut its doors on 18 February 2023, blaming a decline in footfall through the station.

Just as had happened with the Square, there had soon been complaints about the state of the station. Almost every aspect of the building apart from its 'general perspective' was criticised in the *Huddersfield Chronicle* in 1857 and in 1880 the same newspaper made use of quotes from a *Leeds Mercury* columnist, 'Jackdaw', who had remarked that the station's 'imposing external appearance is its only redeeming feature'.

...The first-class and ladies waiting rooms are anything but first-class in accommodation and appointment; and the sanitary arrangements are a positive disgrace to the entire management... Nay, for a station of such pretension, this provision is the worst we ever saw, and we doubt its parallel could be found. Almost without ventilation and deficient of light, the places are positively nauseous; for, as if to add to the intensity of the evil arising from the original mal-arrangement, the places – where constant cleanliness is indispensable – are left in a filthy state of neglect...

Huddersfield Chronicle,
29 August 1857

...If a passenger wearies of the sight and seeks repass in the waiting room, he is met with a picture of discomfort which "Jackdaw" would describe as filthy, while discordant uproar highly offensive to the sensitive ear proceeds from shrill whistles, shouts of porters, imprecations of rough passengers, and perhaps the hubbub of excursionists and marketing people that crowd the booking-office and their approaches.

Huddersfield Chronicle,
2 October 1880

Perhaps some of these criticisms were redressed when the interior of the station was rebuilt in 1886. The improvements included a new central booking-office with waiting-rooms on either side; the construction of the island platform and a subway; staff offices and a porters' room; telegraph and refreshment-rooms as well as lavatories.

By 1861 Huddersfield's first station master William Padmore had moved to a new house in Fartown, and soon after left the town altogether when he was

Station manager Angie Hunte with station cat Bolt in July 2022, courtesy Transpennine Express.

promoted to be the station master at Crewe, one of the busiest junctions on the network. The timepiece he was given to mark his departure was inscribed with the words: 'Presented along with a purse containing 40 sovereigns by a number of the inhabitants of Huddersfield, to Mr William Padmore, who for nearly 15 years filled the office of station master at the London and North Western Railway, Huddersfield, with civility, promptitude and integrity'. In his response Padmore replied that the 'time-piece' would be kept as a 'family memorial of the kindness of the inhabitants of Huddersfield towards me'. Padmore was the only station master to live at the station but a later stationmaster, F.W. Brereton, who retired in 1931, became well known not only because of the length of his service but also for his dress-style and his dog.

...Mr Brereton had been stationmaster at Huddersfield for twenty years when he retired. He began his career on the railway in 1882 as a junior porter at Handsworth, and later held positions as a signalman and as district inspector at Exchange Station, Manchester.

Mr Brereton never wore a stationmaster's uniform, but when he was on duty was always attired in a frock coat and top hat, as was at one time customary for station-masters throughout the country. He was usually accompanied on the station platform by his dog, Jack, which carried on its back a collecting box for the Railway Benevolent Institution.

Leeds Mercury, 18 May 1933

However, it must be said, that the fame of the present residents of the station has spread far beyond Huddersfield; station 'pest controllers' Felix and Bolt have a large following on social media and Felix has even been the subject of a book featured on the *Sunday Times*' best-seller list.

It is now difficult to believe that Huddersfield Station might not look as it does today but in the 1960s British Rail had started to sell off property and the front of Huddersfield Railway Station was amongst sites being considered for redevelopment. Clifford Stephenson, a former Huddersfield Borough Alderman, recalled how the station front was saved from demolition in 1968, the Centenary of Huddersfield's Incorporation as a Borough.

To celebrate the Centenary, the Finance Committee reserved £100,000 to provide some kind of permanent memorial, not defined. Suggestions were invited; many were received...I, somewhat tentatively, put forward again my earlier proposal to buy the Station, this time, in the absence of a rival alternative and with time running out for a decision to be made, it was agreed that purchase be negotiated. Shortly afterwards three of us met Mr Fiennes, the manager of British Rail North East Region, in the Mayor's parlour, to discuss the purchase. I never took part in a transaction so speedy and amicable...For a mere £52,650 Huddersfield became the owner of the Station Front Buildings, platform 1 and the rail track adjoining it, together with the forecourt - now used for car parking. I think it was a bargain financially and architecturally, a treasure beyond price...

The rent received from British Rail for use of the buildings and the income from car parking, together, now more than pay the debt charges incurred by the purchase, so, in effect Huddersfield became the owner of this splendid monument of the great railway age, for nothing, and in the process notched up another 'first' as the only town to own its main railway station.

Clifford Stephenson, 'Buying a Station' in
Huddersfield Local History Society, *Journal*, Spring 1991

A 'treasure beyond price'? Sir John Betjeman who once described Huddersfield railway station as having the 'most splendid façade' of any railway station in England would probably have agreed. Certainly, the station's façade came as a complete surprise to train driver Nick Tozer when he first arrived in Huddersfield.

I've worked around the country at a number of depots. I was at Charing Cross, which was another beautiful station but small in comparison, but that morning in 1988 when I walked around the corner and the sun was shining at the front. It was a 'wow' moment. I'm not exaggerating, it was one of those rare wow moments that you felt good about going to a place...I still think it's a fantastic frontage. When they put Harold out front, that was one of the best things they could have done. I think it's just so right.

NICK TOZER, May 2023

Mental health charity Platform 1's Pacer train being lifted into position, July 2021, courtesy Martin Shaw.

OPENING OF THE RAILWAY FROM HUDDERSFIELD TO COOPER BRIDGE

On Monday last the town of Huddersfield was again all life and activity in consequence of the formal opening of the Cooper Bridge and Manchester Railway, now incorporated with the London and North Western...At ten minutes to twelve o' clock the first train consisting of about 12 carriages started and arrived at the junction in ten minutes. The first-class carriages were chiefly occupied by the directors and the shareholders and their families, and the remainder by a portion of the respectable inhabitants of Huddersfield and its vicinage, who had availed themselves of the opportunity of enjoying the novelty the first and gratuitous trip afforded. The engine was driven by Mr Reach, the manager of the engine department, and the train ran with perfect steadiness. On arriving at the junction, Joseph Brook, Esq, the vice-chairman, named the engine "The Aldam" by dashing a bottle of champagne onto it... [Mr Brook gives short address] ...Three cheers were then given for the success of the undertaking, and the train amidst the shouts of the passengers, and the playing of music. On the train reaching the station, it was received with loud huzzas. The line was then considered to be formally opened, the bands playing "God save the Queen." At two o'clock dinner was served at the station to about 600 of the workmen, and the directors and engineers afterwards dined together at the George Hotel...The opening of this line of railway may be said to be the commencement of a new era in the history of the town of Huddersfield...

Morning Herald, 5 August 1847

ARRIVING IN THE SQUARE

TWO YEARS LATER the opening of the line westwards to Liverpool provided the opportunity to run the 'First Excursion train on the Huddersfield & Manchester Railway' with a Special Train from Leeds to Liverpool on 14 August 1849. Today arriving and departing from the Station has become part of many people's daily routine but for others over the years, their first view of Huddersfield has been St George's Square.

New arrivals had played their part in Huddersfield's history long before the first train steamed into town in 1847 but the coming of the railway brought more people to the town, many first arriving here in search of work. Amongst those who followed their job here was auditor James Albert Woolven - arriving in 1873 he became landlord of the Bull and Mouth and a wine and sprit merchant, serving as an Alderman and as Mayor of Huddersfield between 1919 and 1921. Many came to Huddersfield to work in the mills and factories but amongst those who arrived by train were young women from other parts of the country to take up work in the homes of well-to-do Huddersfield residents. Those who took these servant jobs mostly came from areas where agriculture and coal mining predominated and employment options for women were limited. Looking out onto St George's Square they would not be able to miss Lion Buildings which housed the 'Head Registry', a recruitment agency for servants, advertising in newspapers as far afield as Stamford and St Helens. Adverts placed by the Registry in 1901 claimed it had been in existence for fifty years. In the 1930s Lion Chambers could still be a place to go for those looking for work, although of a different kind. Cotto Washing Machines advertised three vacancies for 'Salesmen' (*Huddersfield Daily Examiner*, 26 October 1934) but ladies with sales experience would also be considered; applicants were invited to apply in person to 9 Lion Chambers.

SERVANTS (good) wanted for Yorkshire. Good wages. Comfortable homes –Miss Hellawell, Head Registry, Lion-arcade, Huddersfield.

Stamford Mercury,
19 June 1896

Two of the three paintings which comprised Kevin Threlfall's 175 Years of Arrival on display at Huddersfield Railway Station, 21 August 2022 (Photo by Laura Mateescu, courtesy of Let's Go Yorkshire).

From the early 1960s people coming from the Indian sub-continent arrived at the Station as a consequence of the 1947 Partition and in response to requests for labour in the town's mills. Some of those early arrivals have talked about their experiences in a moving film, *A New Life in Huddersfield*, As Mandeep Samra, who directed the film, explains: 'The human impact of partition was incalculable and has resonated through time and place to where we live now in Huddersfield.'

Men like Mohammed and Mansaf would arrive in Huddersfield first to find work as well as somewhere to live with their families following them to Britain later.

I came in 1961. It was very difficult to get a passport in those days. My uncle, he said, go to Huddersfield. There are plenty of mill jobs there. We got off at Huddersfield Station. English lady, she came in. She got a taxi for us. I found UK totally different. Houses, they looked different and every house, they had smoke, you see, chimneys. Every day we had to light our own fire with coal, and then go to work.

Mohammed Anif Assad

It was a very exciting journey. We came out of the train. We came out in St George's Square. There was a collector here on the gate collecting the tickets. Before he asked me for my ticket, I said, 'We want to go to Bath Street. Can you help me to get a taxi please?' He said, 'You don't need a taxi because I live there, same street and I'm finishing work. I'll take you with me. People were very, very helpful. And as soon as we got to the house it was very foggy. We couldn't see anything'.

Mansaf Ali

From *A New Life in Huddersfield*, 2017
(Produced by Let's Go Yorkshire; Director: Mandeep Samra)

Mandeep Samra has told the story in words and pictures of her father Kulbir's journey from being a small boy in a village in West Panjab to his arrival in Huddersfield in 1963 and making a new life here. Kulbir was able to tell his friend that 'his town was the most beautiful in the world'. But it is also the story of how people like Kulbir were caught up in the Partition of the Indian sub-continent in 1947 and its aftermath.

Although people had come from Ireland to find work and settle in the town long before the railway came, this was still the case in June 1956

The *'most beautiful town in the world'*, illustration from Mandeep Samra's The Boy Who Lost His Home But Carried Light, *2023, published by Let's Go Yorkshire.*

when Laura Lambe arrived at the station with her mother and two siblings. Laura's mother had told her children they were going to start a new life in Huddersfield, but she still remembers how disappointed she was by her first view of the town, and of the Square. But, despite her initial misgivings, Laura did make a life for herself in Huddersfield.

I couldn't wait to see Huddersfield as my mother brought her three very tired children with all our belongings and luggage onto the steps of the station, seemingly engulfed between two huge pillars on either side of us as we looked out into the Square before us. This was summertime but there was no sun shining, no beautiful buildings, no fine ladies or gents, no wonderful cars or even birds singing in the Square. Not a sign of life anywhere before us.

My heart sank with feelings of shock, disbelief, bewilderment as I looked out on the bleak, lifeless, old soot-covered buildings around this Square as it might have been in years gone by. How much soot and grime did it take to cover these buildings, I asked myself, as I tried to suppress my tears for the sake of my family? This was so disappointing and added to my feelings of isolation and abandonment as we stood there alone, no one to welcome us as my father was at work.

But no time for regrets as the taxi driver bundled us and the luggage into a black cab, speaking in a very strange language/tongue to my mother, calling her 'luv', saying, 'Eh lass, where's thou going? Hast thou got some brass?' and to me, 'What's up? Ain't so bad'. Another shock, surely we were not going to have to learn a new language? I couldn't wait to leave this Square in which my dreams had been shattered on what should have been the happiest and most exciting day of my life.

LAURA LAMBE, January 2023

Train in station, courtesy Kirklees Image Archive.

In December 1969 Lee Hong Hirst arrived at Huddersfield station following a long journey from Penang in Malaysia. Lee Hong was one of many young Malaysian women who arrived at that time to work in the NHS as Huddersfield Royal Infirmary went out of its way to recruit student nurses from Malaysia. After completing her training, Lee Hong stayed here, working as a midwife and delivering several generations of Huddersfield and Halifax citizens. Like Laura before her, Lee Hong's arrival at the Station was not quite as she expected.

After the tropics of Malaysia the cold weather was a bit of a shock and so was finding out there was no one to meet me at the station. I had to put the unfamiliar coins I possessed into the station telephone and call the hospital, because I had no idea where to go. The call worked and shortly afterwards I was standing in St George's Square, on the station steps, waiting for the taxi that took me to Huddersfield Royal Infirmary. So began my 46-year career working in the NHS, mostly as a midwife. I have delivered many babies in Huddersfield and Halifax over the years and in some cases have supported women from more than one generation of a family. As a result I am often recognised. When this happens, I am moved by the lovely things people say to me.

Something which made me feel welcome when I arrived in Huddersfield was the friendly way people addressed me. The warden at the nurses' home welcomed me with 'Hello Love' and this was a big contrast to how I had been spoken to in London. Although, I do remember that despite her friendly manner, the warden was strict and would lock out any student nurse who dared to stay out later than 10pm.

LEE HONG HIRST, August 2022

And there were those who came to Huddersfield because they were fleeing from war. A crowd of around 5,000 gathered around the station in October 1914 to welcome the first party of Belgian refugees. As the *Examiner* reported: 'Every point of vantage was taken up by the crowd. Some boys stood on the top of taxi-cabs, and the large number of motor-cars provided by members of the Huddersfield Automobile Club for the conveyance of the refugees provided convenient platforms for the owners and their friends. There was much cheering as the train drew into the station, and this was renewed outside as the refugees and their bundles were got into the motor-cars and driven away. Some of the women refugees particularly were visibly affected by the cordiality of their reception' (*Huddersfield Daily Examiner*, 8 October 1914).

Huddersfield has continued to welcome people from many countries who have lost their homes and families and Sanctuary Kirklees is part of the national City of Sanctuary movement.

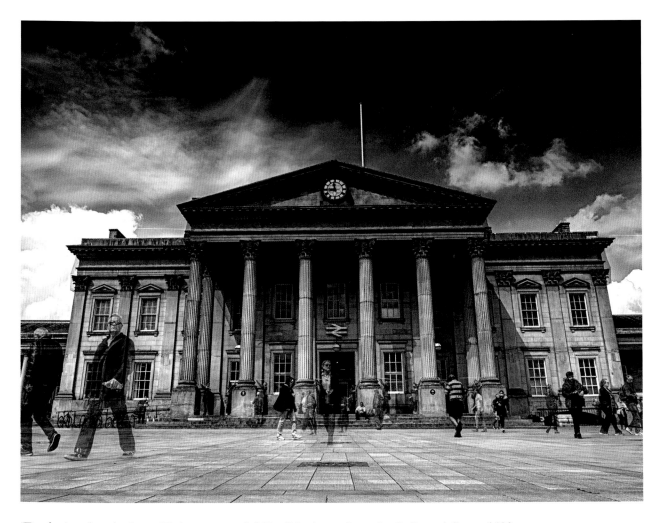

'Timeless', a photo by Roger Kinder, was awarded First Prize in our Capturing St George's Square 2020 - 2022 competition. The judges felt that the image provided 'a reminder of the countless many who have flowed through the station entrance over the decades.'

...AND
DEPARTURES

NETHERLANDS MAIL STEAMERS

£2 10s. – £2 10s. – £2 10s

HUDDERSFIELD to NEW YORK or PHILADELPHIA, entire fare £2 10s (infants free), including excellent provisions and separate sleeping berths in enclosed cabins. Privacy, speed and comfort make this a favourite route for English families with limited means. Passengers leave Huddersfield, every Wednesday. Through tickets from Huddersfield to all stations in the United States now reduced. Buenos Ayres and all River Plate Ports from Huddersfield, £8. Levy's Shipping Offices, 41, Finsbury Pavement, London

Huddersfield Daily Examiner, 13 September 1886

THERE ARE ALSO many reasons why people have passed through the station and the Square when leaving Huddersfield, some to begin a new life elsewhere. Before the First World War it would have been difficult to open a local newspaper and not find an advert aimed at anyone considering emigration and giving details of an agent in the town. The Netherland Mail Steamers company even offered station-to-station tickets and the Huddersfield Parcels Company with an office in Railway Street claimed to be 'officially appointed agents for Assisted and Nominated Passages to the Colonies'. And there are many like Jenny who left their family in Huddersfield to begin the next stage

> On 7 September 1962, at the tender age of 17, I said goodbye to my parents in the Square outside Huddersfield Railway Station to travel to Spitalgate, Near Grantham, in Lincolnshire to start a new life in the WRAF. This was a momentous occasion for me, and the environment and mixed emotions are indelibly printed on my memory.
>
> JENNY NOAKE, July 2022

in their life but most departures from the Square have been less momentous and have often been in pursuit of leisure.

While the cost of the first railway excursions from Huddersfield would have been beyond the means of most working class people, it would be difficult to overestimate the importance of the railway in providing opportunities to travel. As early as 1853 the LNWR were advertising Whitsuntide Holidays excursions. Alongside an excursion from 'Huddersfield to London and back' for 17 shillings, offering travellers the chance to return within four or 13 days, the railway company also advertised an 'Annual Treat to the Working Classes. Marcus's Cheap Trip. Huddersfield to Liverpool and Back for five shillings.' H. R. Marcus was described as 'Manager and Conductor of Excursion Trains to the London and North Western Railway'. A number of sights that Huddersfield people might want to visit were listed, including the 'Blind Asylum' and the Sailors' Home but also New Brighton, a seaside resort

A party from Kirkheaton before setting off for Blackpool, courtesy Kirklees Image Archive.

across the Mersey. Stan Sagan has told us that, more than a century later, his first train journey from Huddersfield was to New Brighton.

In addition to adverts for excursions, there were regular reports of people making the most of the Huddersfield Holidays by taking train trips which could even lead to crowds in the Square.

THE HOLIDAYS
Busy Scene at Huddersfield Railway Station
MORE HEAVY BOOKINGS

Animated scenes have predominated at Huddersfield during the weekend, and the passenger traffic has been exceedingly heavy. As was indicated in the 'Examiner' on Friday and Saturday there were advance bookings by Saturday's excursion trains aggregating over 7,000, and from an early hour that morning and for several hours during the forenoon there were huge crowds in St George's Square. Excellent order prevailed, and the traffic was disposed of by the railway officials smartly and without mishap...

Huddersfield Daily Examiner, 5 September 1921

The most popular excursions from Huddersfield in 1921 organised by LNWR were to Belle Vue for the brass band contest, Liverpool, Scarborough, Bridlington and Filey while the L&YR had 400 advance bookings to Blackpool and 150 for Southport. According to railway officials 1939 was a record year with thousands queuing in the Square on Saturday 12 August, waiting for 56 trains bound for seaside resorts: 'It is estimated that between twenty and thirty thousand people left the town over the weekend, and that at least 15,000 of these left by train' (*Leeds Mercury*, 14 August 1939). Just 23 days later, the country was once again at war with Germany. The Square and the station continued to be a point of departure during the Huddersfield Holiday but with less reliance on excursion trains.

I have a happy childhood memory of walking from the bus stop on Lord Street to the train station in St George's Square holding my mum's hand. My dad was carrying our luggage, helped by my older brother, and we were setting off on our annual week away. My dad worked at Hopkinson's engineering works, so like many of the other families waiting on the station platform, we went away during the Huddersfield fortnight, which coincided with the beginning of the six-week school holiday. At that time there was a direct train to North Wales from Huddersfield, and Llandudno was our destination. The train had compartments like the Hogwarts Express depicted in the Harry Potter novels. As I looked out of the window, eager to see the first glimpse of the sea, it certainly felt magical to me.

BEVERLEY NORRIS, February 2023

I've met many a time in the Square over the years to go on race trips, Blackpool trips and stag dos. These were all made easy as coaches could park without difficulty in those days. Alas, things change and now the Square is a place to meet before jumping on a train to go further afield but it is still a place to leave from as in the past.

JEFF MELLOR, March 2022

Other memories of the Square are of exciting family journeys by train, starting from Huddersfield Railway Station. Both my grandfathers worked on the railway, so we went everywhere by train. Happy times!

SALLY BARBER, October 2022

As Jeff Mellor remembers, the Square has always provided a starting point for journeys:

The Square has always been a meeting point for people with somewhere to go. I have a couple of postcards addressed to my Dad from the secretary, Leonard Oldham, of the Huddersfield Billiards and Snooker Association to confirm my thoughts. He was informed that he had been selected to play for Huddersfield in the Yorkshire League and to meet in the square. This goes back to the early 1950s and the Huddersfield Snooker and Billiards team would go on a coach along with their supporters to away matches leaving from the Square.

In 1979 the Colne Valley representative side met in the Square to go to Germany to play in a football tournament and returned four days later with their trophies after a successful trip. During the 1980s many football teams met in the Square on a Saturday lunch time before jumping into their cars and heading off to their games. Parking wasn't as restrictive as it is now.

JEFF MELLOR, March 2022

Colne Valley football team 1979, courtesy Jeff Mellor.

The Square has also provided a useful point for those setting off on cycle rides and walks – Jean has told us that in the past members of Huddersfield Rucksack Club used to meet on the steps of Huddersfield Building Society and Katie remembers that the Square was the starting point for a walk up Castle Hill with the Huddersfield Ramblers. Today many Discover Huddersfield walks start from Harold Wilson's statue but some societies, meeting in the Square, may have been less energetic:

Members of Huddersfield Coffee Pot Society, the social group for those in their 20s and 30s, would often muster on the station steps and sort transport arrangements for the planned evening. A number of us still meet up. Now 60s, 70s and 80s!!

ADRIAN LEE, March 2022

The Thespians, having won first prize in a British Drama League's competition, setting off for New York in 1926 to take part in a competition for amateur theatre groups. They came second! Courtesy, Huddersfield Thespians and WYAS Kirklees.

AT THE GEORGE

THE GEORGE HOTEL – A GREAT PAST AND A GLORIOUS FUTURE?

BRIAN HAIGH

THE NEW GEORGE HOTEL was the first building to be erected on the square in front of the recently opened railway station. Designed by William Wallen for the Ramsden Estate, it set a standard for future development in the area.

Like the railway station, it was built by Joseph Kaye who brought in the cheapest tender. He was able to use stone left over from the station and had

The George Hotel, showing tramlines, courtesy Kirklees Local Studies Library.

sufficient men on his books that work could begin without delay. Excavation of the foundations began in March 1849, barely a month after the opening of the tenders. Despite a severe winter, the builders had started constructing the upper storey in February 1850. Across the road, at the corner of Brook Street, on the site of a former brickyard, work began on the hotel's stabling. This was at an additional cost of £720. The final cost of the new hotel was £10,374 10s 7d, more than £4000 over the original estimate. This was put down to changes from the original plans and decorative features.

Thomas Wigney, who had been at the old George Inn in the Market Place, took on the tenancy and the first guests were welcomed on 27 August 1851. He was succeeded by other members of the family who are celebrated in an obelisk which survives in St Peter's Gardens.

Whilst the Wigneys were to complain that trade was not as good, probably a ploy to secure rent reductions, under their successors standards were said to have fallen to a level that was unbefitting of the town's premier hotel. Seeing an opportunity, in 1872 a group of Huddersfield businessmen formed a limited company to take over the lease; running the hotel has been in corporate hands ever since. The George Hotel Co. Ltd. brought in Huddersfield architect W.H. Crossland to make alterations and additions including new kitchens and a laundry. Furnishings were supplied by cabinet-makers Brown & Lamont of Chester. On the eve of the First World War, another local architect Willie Cooper was responsible for a complete refurbishment which included furniture from Waring & Gillow. When the freehold was bought by Huddersfield Corporation in 1920 as part of the Ramsden Estate there were 45 bedrooms, some with private sitting rooms, a restaurant, billiard room and other facilities as well as stabling.

In one of the ground floor rooms, later to become the home of the popular Tudor Bar, what was to become the Rugby League was formed in the last week of August 1895. Compensation for broken time had been a major topic for debate by English rugby's governing body but when the matter came to the vote in 1893, it was roundly defeated. The Rugby Football Union stressed the amateur nature of the game which it was argued should continue to be governed from headquarters in London. This was unacceptable to many of the northerners and the clubs which they represented. A series of meetings followed at the Spread Eagle on Corporation Street in Manchester and at Huddersfield's George Hotel, convenient for members from either side of the Pennines. At the meeting at the George on 25 August, the representatives of twelve Yorkshire and nine Lancashire clubs took the momentous decision to break away from the RFU, form a northern union and established the principle of payment for broken time. From September, when the new season got underway, players were able to claim six shillings (30p) provided they could show that they had lost a day's pay.

James Mason was a lifelong supporter of 'Fartown' (Huddersfield RLFC) though as a young man he could not wait to get away from the town of his birth. In later years, family and business brought him back to the town which had grown in his affection. On his many visits, he became a regular at the George which in the fifties and sixties was at the heart of the town's social life. James, later Lord, Hanson added a touch of glamour, entertaining his many friends including his one time fiancée Audrey Hepburn. Sir Malcolm Sargent stayed at the hotel on his visits to conduct the Huddersfield Choral Society. Lunch clubs, charity dinners, wedding breakfasts, annual dinners and dances were a regular feature of the social diary.

But fashions were changing. Town centre hotels with limited parking had to compete with the new venues that were springing up. Successive managements of the George failed to modernise the accommodation and invest in new facilities. After more than one near miss, the inevitable happened. The receivers were called-in in 2013 and the doors of the George were locked. A sale was soon agreed to local dentist and entrepreneur, Dr Altaf Hussain, who announced ambitious plans to re-develop the hotel to include some apartments and a roof top lounge bar. Start dates for the work came and went – a matter of great concern for many local people, who witnessed the gradual deterioration of the building. It was an embarrassment to the local authority which considered St George's Square a key gateway to the town and the George an important element in the recently published Town Centre Blueprint.

In March 2020, it was announced that Kirklees Council had agreed terms for the purchase of the building as part of the regeneration programme. The purchase came as the coronavirus crisis set in but work has now started on this much-loved town centre building. There is much at stake. In 1851, the new hotel set the standard for the development of the area; a flagship re-development of the George could help to kickstart the town's regeneration.

* * *

WHILE FIGURES AVAILABLE from Census Returns (*Table 1*) suggest that the bedrooms available at the George seemed generally to be underoccupied before World War Two, what is without doubt is that the George has played a significant role in the life of our town, playing host to a wide variety of functions and a place for societies to meet as well as to eat and drink. It was the usual meeting place for the Trustees of the various Turnpike Roads that surrounded the town, not to mention bankruptcy creditors' meetings and events in the Square were often followed by large banquets with hotel keepers frequently praised in the local press for the quality of the 'repasts' they had provided.

Table 1: Summary of Census returns for the George Hotel 1861-1939

YEAR OF CENSUS	HOTEL KEEPER, PROPRIETOR, MAN-AGER	FAMILY MEMBERS	SERVANTS	LODGERS, VISITORS
1861	Thomas Jennings Wigney	5	12	15 (including family of 5 & their servant)
1871	Richard Nutter	4	10	6
1881	Mary A. Botting	4	20 (including bookkeeper)	7
1891	R. Jackson Heap	4	25 (including the George Tap Room)	2
1901	John Johnson	5	18	2
1911	John Johnson	6	21	3
1921 (June)	Kate Ducksbury / Harry Ducksbury	2	14	20
1939 Register (Sept)	Harry Ducksbury (managing-director, hotel company)	2	17	14

Some of those who managed the George could now be described as hospitality professionals – Harry Ducksbury's father had been a 'hotel proprietor' moving between large hotels – Wigney and Nutter also traded as Wine and Spirit Merchants and both owned farms. Commercial travellers frequently stayed at the hotel, sometimes bringing their wives, as did textile manufacturers.

TRAVELLERS BANQUET. - The first annual banquet of the wholesale woollen travellers and salesmen of Huddersfield took place at the George Hotel, last night week. Nearly 40 partook of a sumptuous repast, served in Mr and Mrs Nutter's well-known style of excellence...The loyal toasts were afterwards given as were also the "Town and trade of Huddersfield", the "Woollen travellers and salesmen of Huddersfield", "the Ladies" &c. Singing and other entertainments filled up an agreeable evening.

Huddersfield Chronicle,
7 September 1871

Dancing was also an entertainment that could be found at the George but one imagines that the type of 'dancing and exercises' offered by the Leeds-based Misses Jacksons' Academy on Thursday mornings in 1874 were very different from the style of dance in September 1940 when Harry Ducksbury applied to extend the hotel's dancing licence. Ducksbury's application was opposed by Superintendent Chadwick from the Borough Police. In the 1970s dinner dances were all the rage and an advert in December 1974 declared that 'the best way to thank your wife for Christmas Dinner is to eat out'.

In addition to the improvements that had already been made by the George Hotel Co. Ltd., a restaurant was opened on the ground floor opposite the station in 1888. This was not enough for several Huddersfield councillors who thought the town was important enough to have its own railway hotel: Manchester, Bradford, Newcastle and York were all mentioned. The two railway companies refused to consider the suggestion, stating in a letter to the Council that it was a 'matter rather for private enterprise, and beyond their scope as railway companies' (*Huddersfield Chronicle*, 23 December 1893). The company ceased to lease the hotel in 1897. Other changes were made to the hotel over the years; in September 1991 Lord Hanson visited the hotel

Billheads used by the George, courtesy WYAS Kirklees.

HOTELS £20,000 PLAN

Alterations to the George Hotel,- in St George's Square, Huddersfield, to cost £20,000, include a new dining-room and an enlarged ballroom, together with screened lighting in the American Bar. The building is owned by the Huddersfield Corporation, and the licensee is Mr H. L. Ducksbury.

Yorkshire Observer, 4 February 1938.

***

BAR ATTENDANTS required for gentlemen's smoke room. – George Hotel, Huddersfield. Tel. 5000.

Yorkshire Post, 9 April 1955.

---

to unveil a plaque celebrating a £1 million refurbishment by the Principal Hotels group. A two-night 'Flexibreak' at the George, advertised in 1993, could be had for £60 per person per night including a 'private bathroom', a full English breakfast and a three-course evening meal with children under 13 staying for free.

There was a time during the Second World War when the George was definitely the place to go for a meal; in one week in December 1940 the hotel obtained nearly three times its permitted meat ration (*Yorkshire Observer*, 1 July 1941). The George was again in the news in September 1948 when a fire, which sent 50 people running out, was reported in the national press. The *Yorkshire Observer* could not help but report that 'women scantily dressed in silk "nighties" and dressing gowns and men in pyjamas shivered in the cold as they waited for cars to take them from outside the George Hotel to the warmth and shelter of the Huddersfield police office'. Nobody was injured. But there were also good news stories – in 1948 a dog belonging to Agnes O'Sullivan who served cocktails in the American Bar won the Irish Coursing Derby and Elizabeth Booth was named as Britain's top hotel receptionist in 1970.

However, there is one event with which the George will be for ever associated:

THE RUGBY FOOTBALL CRISIS ESTABLISHMENT OF THE NORTHERN FOOTBALL UNION

A meeting of the representatives of 20 important Rugby Football Clubs in Yorkshire and Lancashire was held at the George Hotel, Huddersfield, on Thursday evening, for the purpose of formally establishing the Northern Rugby Football Union...[lists names of those present representing the Clubs]. After full discussion, which took place in private, it was decided to form a Northern Rugby Football Union on the principle of payment for bona fide broken time only. Stockport were admitted members of the union. The resignation from the English Rugby Union was handed in from 20 clubs, Dewsbury being the exception. It was resolved that each club represented at the meeting should sign a membership list, with the exception of Dewsbury, who were given till Tuesday to decide.

Huddersfield Daily Chronicle, 30 August 1895

The George has had many sporting connections – a home team's triumphant return to the town would often end with a celebratory meal at the George and visiting teams would often stay at the hotel. The Australians pictured opposite look to be enjoying themselves outside the George while visiting Huddersfield during the 1973 Kangaroos Tour; they easily defeated Huddersfield 2-32 at Fartown on 10 November.

Many will remember visiting the Rugby League Heritage Centre in the basement of the George which consisted of memorabilia ranging from programmes to jerseys collected by former player and Sky Sports commentator Mike 'Stevo' Stephenson. His collection has now found a home in the University of Huddersfield's Heritage Quay

Despite the hotel's fluctuating fortunes over the years, as we have seen it was still the place where the famous tended to stay. It was music that brought many to Huddersfield and to the George – from reggae stars such as Jimmy Cliff and Desmond Dekker to avant-garde composer Karlheinz Stockhausen who took part in the 1988 Huddersfield Contemporary Music Festival.

'Stevo's Bar' - poster found in the George, 2021.

Australian rugby league team outside George during 1973 tour, courtesy Kirklees Local Studies Library.

Back in the eighties I was out for a meal with my mum at the George Hotel when Gorden Kaye and Su Pollard walked past our table. They must have been dining in the restaurant and were leaving. Both were actors in successful sitcoms at the time, Su Pollard in Hi-De-Hi! and Gorden Kaye in 'Allo 'Allo! I remember Su Pollard was very friendly and was speaking to people who recognised her, but Gorden Kaye was quieter. My mum had known Gorden when he was a child and they lived on the same street in Moldgreen.

STEPHEN CLEGG, September 2021

We have held rugby reunions there every two years, obviously when it was up and running but it was rugby union, not rugby league, so I think perhaps we were doing that as a little bit of a prod because we were in the dining area where there were all the pictures of the Rugby League formation in the George Hotel which we all knew about of course so it was a bit of fun really. When the hotel closed down, or even before that I think, we found it necessary to move...

IAN STEPHENSON, January 2023

But for many, their memories of the George relate to the part the hotel has played in their own personal history.

St George's Square reminds me of the George Hotel, where I celebrated my wedding reception almost 40 years ago. We stayed there overnight on our wedding night. The next morning, after checking out, we went to our car parked in St George's Square to find it had a flat battery. A friend came to the rescue.

SALLY BARBER, October 2022

My first marriage, August 1968, and the Reception was held at the George which was considered to be quite posh in those days and it was lovely.

IAN STEPHENSON, January 2023

In 2021, eight years after the George closed its doors, the scaffolding went up so the renovation of its exterior could begin, and as this book is being put together, the scaffolding has been dismantled and work has started on restoring the interior.

Helen Walker, Conservation Architect and Head of Heritage, Bowman Riley, at work, courtesy Kirklees Council.

Interior of the George before renovation, courtesy Alan Stopher, Huddersfield Photo-Imaging Club.

OPENING OF THE "LION ARCADE"

Rarely has an event occurred of a more pleasing interest to our townsmen or, as regards the appearance of Huddersfield, of greater importance, and seldom have we, as journalists had to chronicle any circumstances more really deserving and demanding notice, than that about which so much anxiety is expressed and such lively interest manifested in all circles, - the progress and completion of the Lion Arcade in John William-street...

Mounting the stairs we reach the promenade, extending across the top of the various showrooms facing the grand entrance, ornamented by four pieces of sculpture representing the Seasons, and from which we enter the conservatory of Messrs. Major and Son, of Leeds. In the centre of this plays the fountain; the fine screen in front is that used by Mr Titus Salt of Bradford, at the Great Exhibition; at each end is a private office; and the wall at the back is illuminated by twenty windows. The pillars supporting the ten shops within the arcade imitate Scotch granite; the sashes, which are of brass, enclose immense sheets of plate glass...

Huddersfield Daily Chronicle, 21 January 1854

SHOPPING, SOCIALISING AND SERVICES

THOUSANDS FLOCKED TO the official opening of what was to have been Huddersfield's 'Royal Arcade' but, following the hoisting of the lion onto the roof in February 1853, when a chain broke resulting in some slight grazing to the lion's face, the name Lion Arcade seems to have stuck. At the time of the official opening in January 1854, some of the shops, including a fish and game shop, looked out onto St Peter's Street with a homeopath's on the corner. Facing the Square were Hoyle & Sons' china and glass shop; boot and shoe maker, Mr Varley; Swales the grocer; and a confectioner's shop was also planned. Amongst the businesses reached from inside the building was Mrs Hirst's Registration-office for servants (she also intended to sell cigars and fancy goods) and Miss Ratcliffe's draper's shop. Before moving into the Arcade from her shop in Northgate, Helen Ratcliffe had regularly advertised, keen to inform readers that she was the Huddersfield agent for the Ladies' Industrial Society of Ireland, an organisation which had been set up in 1847 in the wake of the Great Irish Famine to encourage the peasantry to turn to cottage industries. There were also shops for hosiery, paper-hanging and chandeliers, Horsfall and Bailey's music rooms, Mr Priestley's hair-dressing rooms, not to forget Mr Anzani's toy shop. But St George's Square was very much the place to do business and over the shops in the Arcade were several cloth warehouses including that of Oldfield, Allan & Co. The Arcade had been built for Samuel Oldfield, partly to house his company's warehouse, but less than two years after its completion he was bankrupt and it was put up for auction. The successful bid came from none other than Samuel Oldfield himself who said he was bidding on his father's behalf.

In 1855 Henry Tempest was offering fish, oysters, game and poultry in what he described in his adverts as a 'splendid building'. Lion Arcade was, of course, home to a wide range of businesses over the years and photographs

ABOVE LEFT
*Lion Buildings, 1855, from
a brochure advertising an
auction for the building,
courtesy WYAS Kirklees.*

BELOW LEFT
*Lion Buildings, 1968,
courtesy Dave Pattern,
Huddersfield Exposed.*

RIGHT
*Lion Buildings, 2023,
courtesy Stephen Challenger.*

reveal changes both in the building and in our shopping habits. In the early years it would certainly have been a good place to go for linen and other drapery and occasionally those shopping in the Arcade might look across the Square and even spot one of Eddison's horse auctions. For more than 50 years Madame Lucette's was the place to go for ladies' coats, suits and gowns and, if an advert for an apprentice aimed at school-leavers in January 1934 was anything to go by, customers could reasonably expect that the shop assistants could be 'tall, smart and of good appearance.' Next door was Rees Fashions where in 1969 you could also get a winter coat and find a 'large assortment of crimplene dresses'. But one name that certainly stands out in the photos we have seen is that of the Lion Restaurant. In 1950 it was taken over by Hagenbachs, confectioners and bakers, who already had a shop in Market Walk, and even acquired a neon sign! At this time the restaurant could seat 150 people and in 1951 you could lunch there for 2/6d. The Lion Coffee House moved into the same premises in 1988. This too has gone but there is now no shortage of places to eat fronting on to the Square.

Many will remember Wood's Music Shop, either in Market Street or, earlier, in New Street but Joe Wood started with a 'music depot' in Lion Arcade, selling instruments, sheet music and tickets. It was also the place to go to arrange for Mr J. Wood's Quadrille band to play at your event. John North - who became conductor of the Huddersfield Choral, Glee and Madrigal, and Philharmonic Societies as well as choirmaster at Huddersfield Parish Church - started out working as an errand boy with the firm in 1862. Here he was encouraged to develop his musical talent with Wood taking him

PIANO-FORTES & HARMONIUMS.

Purchasers will find it to their advantage to visit

J. WOOD'S MUSIC DEPOT.

ST. GEORGE'S SQUARE, HUDDERSFIELD,

Where is kept the largest Stock of First-class Instruments, by Broadwood, Collard,
Kirkman, and Alexandre, for Sale or Hire on the lowest possible terms.
Second-hand Instruments at all prices from £2. Tuners sent to all parts of the country.

Advertisement from Huddersfield Directory and Year Book, *1868.*

into partnership in 1884. When North died in 1891 his friends recalled a story he used to tell of how he used to practise his violin in the cellar and one of the Arcade tenants pressed a coin into his hands requesting him to stop playing until he had mastered the instrument.

RIGHT
Hairdressers advertising in the Huddersfield Chronicle, *19 February 1872.*

ST. GEORGE'S SQUARE TOILET ROOMS (Established 1853).

The Proprietor of the above Establishment (Mr. H. C. GLEDHILL) desires to offer to the gentry and public generally his grateful acknowledgement of the generous support received during the four months which have elapsed since taking over this business.

Patrons have heartily appreciated the facilities which these Toilet Rooms now afford. Mr Gledhill is, however, anxious to still further increase the business of which these premises are capable, and most respectfully solicits One Visit from those Ladies and Gentlemen who have not yet paid him the honour of a call.

LADIES will find, notwithstanding, an impression to the contrary, that the scale of charges are strictly moderate.

GENTLEMEN will receive nothing but the best Workmanship in these rooms.

CHARGES for Toilet Club will be found most reasonable, varying according to the amount of work required. Estimates supplied on application.

H. C. GLEDHILL
FACING STATION
HUDDERSFIELD

Huddersfield Chronicle, 19 February 1898

The service Harry Gledhill was offering in his 'toilet rooms' was in fact hairdressing. By the time Lion Arcade was open for business, hairdressing establishments were being set up in towns across the country. In January 1855 'Professors Bower and Savile' were advertising their newly opened 'London Hair Dressing and Perfumery Establishment' promising the latest styles. Adverts in the Huddersfield press suggest this was a very competititive business, particularly around St George's Square, and that it was also a trade that offered opportunities to diversify. In 1872 there were three hairdressing businesses very close to each other. Savile no longer called himself 'Professor' and had a sideline selling games and puzzles.

It was probably George Barlow, with a shop and rooms inside the Arcade, who branched out most during his career. In the 1871 census he is described as a hairdresser and toy dealer employing two men, two boys and a girl; his adverts in the same year refer to a 'large toy room open all the year round' as well as cigars. Around 1880 Barlow seems to have moved from selling toys into chiropody with cures for chilblains and ringworm!

By 1956 the only hairdresser to be listed around the Square was Miss Alder who had a Ladies Hairdressing salon at 15 Railway Street. Jeanette, aged 14, started hairdressing in the same building as a Saturday girl in 1972.

I worked there for a lady for about a year quite uneventfully, apart from the fact that it was called Miss Alder's's Coiffure and every time the phone rang I didn't like saying 'Miss Alder's Coiffure'... When I first went there, we had a cellar which was absolutely full of the old hairdressing remedies like Bay Rum, and things like that, I used to have to go and mess about and we used to put wigs on. People who had been poorly used to come and have wigs fitted and have all this Bay Rum treatment and things like that... When the Mayor, Elsie Whitteron, used to come, I was the shampooist and my hands got really bad dermatitis. One day she came in the mayoral car, and she used to park outside the door. When she was going she went to Ralph Cuthbert's, the local chemist at the entrance to the Byram Arcade, and she brought me some cream. She was so concerned about my hands, bless her.

About a year after that a new man [Roger] came to take over the shop and he was a bit of a joker, and he took me on as an apprentice and he used to do some tricks on me. He used to send me across to Estate Buildings to the caretaker there and he used to say, 'Could I fetch him a long stand' so I would find myself stood outside the caretaker's, having asked for a long stand, for about an hour. And then he would send me quite frequently for other things like a glass hammer. What else did he ask me to get him? He used to send me to the butcher's as well which was on Station Street. It's not there any more – that was Mitchell's – for a pound of chicken lips.

JEANETTE, February 2023

Jeanette later returned to work in the same building but by that time, she says, there was no longer a caretaker at Estate Buildings and stationers Coates and Bairstow, which she used to visit, had also gone.

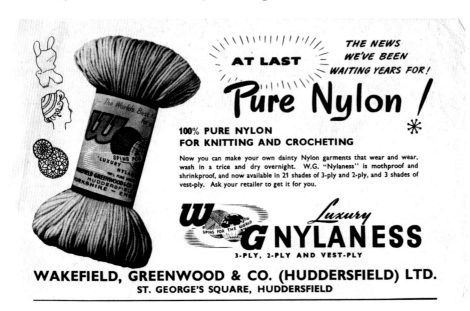

Advertisement from Pins and Needles, *(11, 1952), courtesy* Knitting and Crochet Guild.

Wakefield Greenwood & Co. occupied 6 Railway Street from 1946 to 1960. Set up by Clara Greenwood and her husband Harold Wakefield, the company was a pioneer in introducing new synthetic yarns for hand knitting, including a pure nylon yarn in the early 1950s, and sold knitting wools and other yarns as well as patterns to shops throughout the country, and around the world. Adjacent to Wakefield Greenwood in 1956 was the Huddersfield Parcels Co. but perhaps one of the most surprising organisations to be based in Railway Street was the George Best Fan Club. Ken Stanley, one of the country's first football agents with offices at number 19, counted Denis Law and Best amongst his clients.

The Ramsden Estate Buildings, also in Railway Street, opened 'without ceremony' on 14 August 1870 and housed several other businesses in addition to the Ramsden Estate Office. In 1956, in addition to Huddersfield Corporation Estate offices, the Buildings also housed an auctioneer, two insurance companies, a stock broker, a woollen manufacturer, an estate agent, an accountant, a trades union office, and a taxi business. Estate Buildings is now undergoing extensive repair work and it is hoped that it will be used to provide new homes in the town centre.

As the textile warehouses that surrounded the Square were no longer needed, other businesses, usually requiring less space, moved in. In 1956 no. 7 St George's Square was occupied by a similar range of businesses as those in Estate Buildings, amongst them chartered accountants Revell and Revell.

Revell and Revell began with our great grandfather, Alfred Revell, whose grave can be seen in Edgerton Cemetery. At that time the office was elsewhere in Huddersfield town centre, but at some point it moved to St George's Square as the 'place to be' following the growth of the railways. The business passed down through the family – Harold Revell, Frank Revell, then our father Eric Revell

SYLVIA ARNOLD & ALISON REVELL,
December 2021

Britannia Buildings – built for woollen manufacturers and merchants George Crosland & Sons to provide them with a warehouse, offices and a showroom – was also occupied by more than one company. Crosland had mills in Lockwood and Crosland Moor, and two of his sons became Members of Parliament representing the town – T.P. Crosland between 1865 and 1868 and Sir Joseph Crosland between 1893 and 1895. Before the end of the century the firm had vacated Britannia Buildings and in 1902 the Huddersfield Building Society had moved into the building, moving its headquarters there in 1908, and buying the whole building in 1924. This resulted in a remodelling with the entrance to the Building Society now facing the Square. Various mergers, particularly with the Bradford Building Society, led to changes in names until it became the Yorkshire Building Society.

A home of one's own? Advertisement, County Borough of Huddersfield Directory 1956, *published by Barrett's Publications of Blackpool.*

In 1979 I was newly engaged. My fiancé and I wished to buy a house, but we would need a mortgage. We had savings accounts with The Huddersfield and Bradford Building Society, Britannia Buildings, St George's Square, Huddersfield. We approached the building society to enquire about mortgages. We were disappointed to hear that there was a shortage of mortgages, but would we like to join the waiting list? Yes, please. Most Saturday mornings you would find us in the building society, enquiring about our position on the list. Progress up the list was slow. We would have to wait our turn. I can still remember the delight and excitement, when, one Saturday morning, we were told that we were sufficiently near the top of the list to start house hunting. We bought our first home in April 1980, with the aid of a mortgage from The Huddersfield and Bradford Building Society.

VAL DAVIES, November 2021

But, whatever the name, it is here that many took their first step to acquiring a home of their own although this wasn't always easy. The YBS's St George's Square branch closed in 2005.

The George was not always the only hotel in the Square; Daniel Haigh ran the Cobden Temperance Hotel which, for many years, occupied three storeys fronting into the Square.

THE COBDEN TEMPERANCE HOME AND HOTEL and Boarding House, near Station; 25 bedrooms, clean, new, light, lofty, and spacious. LARGE ROOMS for parties of friends, Public Teas, etc. Sitting Rooms for visitors and boarders. APARTMENTS TO LET.

Front Entrance, St. George's Square, Huddersfield

Huddersfield Daily Examiner
19 July 1888

An animal trainer, Orlando Mocerni, born in the USA, was one of the hotel's six guests on the night of the 1891 Census but by 1911 the temperance hotel, and the Haigh family, had moved to Ramsden Street and then later to Lockwood. The Cobden was certainly more than a place for people to lodge for a night – the Huddersfield Amateur Dramatic Society held a social evening there in October 1895 with musical entertainment and refreshments provided. The temperance tradition was continued in the same building with St George's Temperance Billiard Hall in the basement of the former hotel, opened by H. Wilkinson and G. Taylor in June 1911 with eight state-of-the-art tables but very soon there was competition across the Square from Sloan's Billiard Rooms in the basement of Lion Buildings. There had been previous occupants in the hotel's basement – the Corder restaurant seemed to be notable only for a fire, which was quickly put out but not before it had got the hotel residents out of their beds as well as an 'alleged elopement', both in 1890. At least on one occasion a party of cattle drovers visited the restaurant.

Often places are remembered affectionately because we associate them with a particular time of our lives. This was certainly true of the Alassio coffee bar whose frothy coffee has not been forgotten. And people who remember the Alassio with affection often mention the good food that could be had at the Roma just a few steps away on the corner of Railway Street.

The Alassio Café (in the Tite Buildings opposite Ramsden Estate Buildings) had a great juke box and was one of the few places open on a Sunday.

STAN, August 2022

My mum and stepdad got married at the old Registry Office which was on Railway Street in 1967. This is just off the Square. I remember us coming out into the Square after the wedding. It was near the Alassio Coffee Bar, which I then frequented on Saturday afternoons as a young teenager. We went there for milk shakes after the 'Starlight' Saturday afternoon sessions.

STEPH, February 2023

As teenagers we used to put our hair rollers in and a head scarf and go for a coffee in the Alassio so all the boys knew we were getting ready for a night out in town.

HILARY, June 2022

The Lion Resturant, the Alassio, the Roma and other cafes may have been and gone but other eating places have replaced them in the Square, and you can hear great music at the two pubs which started their lives as booking offices and get a bite to eat after you've got off the train, and sometimes much more!

The Head of Steam pub in St George's Square has been the backdrop to many of my life's events. From works outings and jazz bands to birthday parties and a place to wait before trains to Manchester airport.

It has witnessed the end of romantic relationships and the start of new ones. And on a more prosaic note, has much better toilets than those at the station. Plus the door onto Platform 1 means you can time your departures to perfection, downing your drink as the imminent arrival of your train is announced.

At the time of writing it does a smashing pie and peas with a pint – the perfect tea for winter nights when you have no time to cook.

JANETTE MARTIN, March 2023

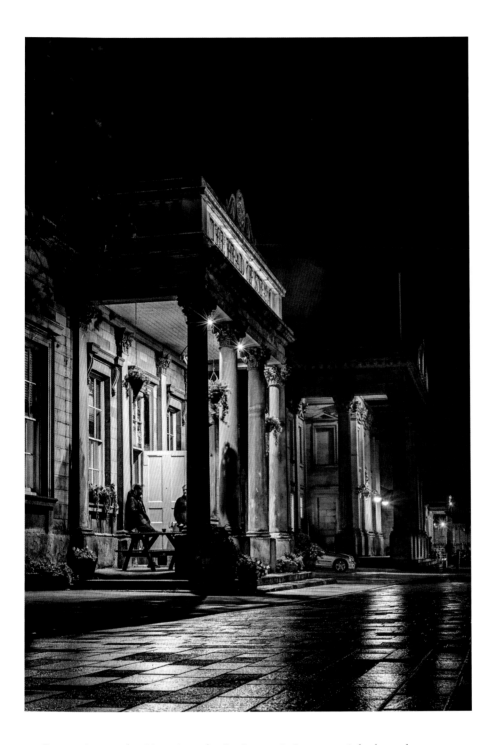

*'The Head of Steam' by
Francis Wilson, runner up,
Capturing St George's Square
2020-2022 photo competition*

Returning to the Lion Arcade, St George's Square might have been a very different place if plans to convert most of the building into a luxury cinema had gone ahead. The proposed Lion Picture House would have had seating for 2532 people, a restaurant and an entrance foyer facing the Square. After

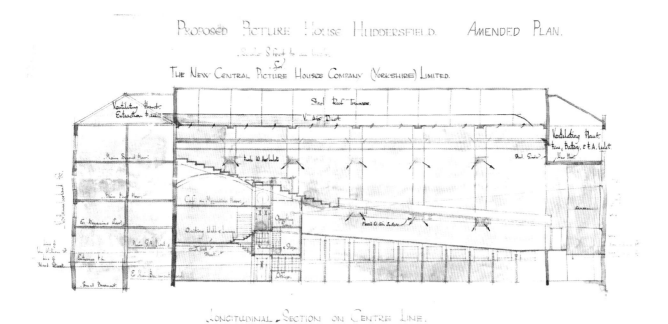

Plan for proposed Picture
House, Lion Buildings,
County Borough of
Huddersfield, Plans approved
7 August 1919, courtesy
WYAS Kirklees.

some modifications, the plans had been approved by the Borough Council,
but the conversion never went ahead because the scheme failed to attract
sufficient investors.

But what better place for a pop-up toy shop? The Electric Palace in 1900
may have anticipated the Christmas markets of recent years but the reference
to the Boer War, with its emphasis on boys' toys, was very much of its time.

At the Children's Christmas Fairy and Electric Palace, which Messrs. H. B. Crawford and
Co. (Limited), 28, Queen-street have opened in St. George's-square, a veritable world in
miniature is presented. Such a magnificent display of toys has never been seen in the
town before. There are no less than 200,000 separate articles, and you can purchase
anything from the half-penny doll to the more costly armoured train, made to wind up
and go. Toy soldiers, including both Britons and Boers, guns, swords, drums, trumpets,
&c., are much in evidence – in fact a whole army of boys could easily be equipped at
this establishment. The show is so vast and varied that it almost defies description, and
must be seen in order to be fully comprehended.

Huddersfield Chronicle, *13 December 1900*

DAVID BLAKEBOROUGH'S MEMORIES OF THE SQUARE

David Blakeborough worked at 7 St George's Square, but his long association with the Square began as a child.

MY EARLIEST MEMORIES of St. George's Square are of catching the route 60 trolleybus from the long bus shelter alongside Railway Street. Smooth, silent buses left every 7 minutes for Birkby, and I alighted at the top of the switchback on Birkby Hall Road to walk up the road to our home higher up the same road. The child fare was one old penny, and the bus tickets were yellow. Beyond the fare stage, tickets were a penny ha'penny (about one new penny) but I never achieved my ambition of getting as far as the terminus!

No 7 St George's Square, courtesy Christine Verguson. The Revell sisters remember the family accountancy business in this building and many law practices have been based here.

Later on, I became a trainspotter. This phrase has now assumed a somewhat derogatory cachet, but back in the 1950s it was Big Stuff, and very popular. We would go to our very grand station to catch trains for Leeds, York, Doncaster and other exotic destinations. There were steam trains then, but if we went to Wakefield by the 7-15am train to change for Doncaster, it was one of the new diesel "multiple units". At that time there was an enquiry office in the area now occupied by the Head of Steam, staffed by a lady with an encyclopaedic knowledge of the British Railways network. The entrance lobby was smaller than it is now, and the ticket office was an art deco wooden structure which had been installed by the London Midland and Scottish Railway, presumably some time between the World Wars. At the age of maybe 12 years I didn't take a great interest in architecture, but I do remember being vaguely puzzled at why anyone would build such a huge magnificent railway station! Now, of course, I know that the Ramsdens wanted something in keeping with the stylish and ambitious new town that they were creating.

Moving on twenty years, having qualified as a solicitor, I applied for and was offered a job as an assistant solicitor at the firm of Brook, Freeman & Co at number 7 St. George's Square. This was one of the oldest solicitors' practices in Huddersfield, having previously been at 47 New Street from where it moved to St. George's Square in about the 1930s. It was originally called Brook Freeman and Batley. The Batley was Joseph Batley, who became the first Town Clerk of the newly incorporated Borough of Huddersfield in 1868.

An office on the corner of St. George's Square and Railway Street, facing the Station, was quite a prestigious location, and in the days before Google Maps and SatNavs it was also quite easy to describe to new clients. The building was owned by some clients of the firm, which may be why they located there. At that time the roundabout was in place together with the "old" Italian fountain, which succumbed to the West Yorkshire weather and was later removed and replaced with a lamp post. Amongst other occupants of the building in 1974 were BM Printers on the first floor along with us, Brian Turner Estate Agent on the ground floor, and in the basement A E Quarmby, tailors.

In 1980 the practice merged with the larger practice of Eaton Smith & Downey, which had previously been located in Britannia Buildings in the Square, but which had moved in 1963 to the newly built Pearl Assurance House on John William Street. However, the premises at 7 St. George's Square were retained, and on the expiration of the lease of Pearl Assurance House the firm moved back to Britannia Buildings, as the office accommodation had been vacated by the Huddersfield and Bradford Building Society. I now had an office overlooking the Square again, this time opposite the George Hotel. I remember seeing Tony Blair unveiling the statue of Harold Wilson in 1999, and before that Her Majesty the Queen arriving in the Royal Train to open the British Amateur Rugby League Association HQ on New North Parade. Eventually Eaton Smith & Downey merged with Marshall Mills & Sykes to become Eaton Smith Marshall Mills, and we moved out of St. George's Square for the final time in, I think, 2000.

'A time for reflection' photographed by Francis Wilson - specially commended in the Capturing St George's Square 2020-2022 photo competition.

CRIME IN
THE SQUARE

SO CONCERNED WAS the Chief Constable with gambling in the 1890s that he ordered St George's Square to be watched around the clock. With so many people passing through the Square and the station as well as frequenting its cafes and hotels, the town's biggest public space certainly provided ample opportunities for both would-be and experienced criminals. The Borough Police Court provided a never-ending stream of stories about a wide range of petty crimes. Using bad language, burglary and begging were amongst the many offences which brought people before the Borough magistrates. Accusations of theft were common, and pickpocketing was a frequent occurrence. There was even a dramatic chase in May 1896 when two police

St. Georges Square   Huddersfield

Young men and boys look towards the camera, postcard, courtesy Christine Verguson

John Radcliffe (18), news lad, Hill Top, Paddock; John Costello (15), shoeblack, Manchester Street; and Herbert Lamb (11), shoeblack, Manchester Street, were charged with playing at pitch and toss at St George's Square, on the 31st ult.– Police-constable Robinson stated that at ten past two on the afternoon in question he saw four or five lads playing at pitch and toss in the square. They were pitching with half-pennies. Costello pitched but did not toss. –Radcliffe pleaded guilty; but Costello said he was not guilty. Lamb did not appear. Mr Ward said that Costello was without parents and lived in a common-lodging house. –The lads were warned about repeating their conduct and were fined 2s 6d including costs.

Supplement to the *Huddersfield Examiner*,
14 February 1891

A NUISANCE IN ST GEORGE'S SQUARE. – John Patrick Swift (15), Boulder's Yard, newsboy, was charged with gambling with coins in St George's-square. Police-constable Appleyard stated that on April 20th he was on duty in St George's-square when he saw the defendant with other lads, tossing with coins. Defendant admitted they were "tossing up to see which would have it." The Chief Constable said the nuisance of gambling in St George's-square was so great that it was found necessary to keep a man constantly stationed there. The boys obtained some money by selling papers, and then gambled for the money. The defendant had been convicted of gambling with cards in October 1889. Defendant was fined 5s., including costs.

Huddersfield Daily Chronicle,
2 May 1891

TRESPASSING AT THE STATION. – James Hill (16), millhand, and Thomas Brook (12), lurry boy, who resided in Upperhead-row, were brought up in custody charged with trespassing on the premises of the railway station. Joseph Vigraas, police-constable at the station, said that the two defendants belonged to a gang of about 40 others who frequented St. George's-square every day in order to pick up odd jobs, such as carrying passengers' luggage, &c. The railway officials kept ordering them away, but on the previous day witness caught the two lads on the top of the steps leading down to the subway. Mr. Green, the station-master, ordered them to be locked up. The defendants promised not to go to the station again, and they were released on their own recognisances to keep the peace for six months.

Huddersfield Daily Chronicle,
11 February 1892

detectives ran across the Square, then jumped into a cab, telling the driver to follow members of a Leeds gang, suspected of pickpocketing, who had been spotted getting off the train. Seeing two of the men in Fountain Street, the detectives jumped out of the cab, and caught up with them in Fitzwilliam Street. One of the men was seen to throw a purse over a wall.

The frequent charges brought against the 'newsboys' working in the Square suggest that they were seen by the police as a problem to be dealt with. 'Newsboys' were certainly not peculiar to Huddersfield and usually came from impoverished backgrounds. Huddersfield's 'newsboys' would probably have spent most of their time in the Square.

Although James and Thomas both state their occupations ('lurry' boys worked for carters), their presence at the station shows that they had to rely on casual work where they could find it. For youths like these, with little money and lots of time, the Square offered opportunities of casual work, petty crime and companionship.

A policeman can be seen to the left of the Peel statue. Postcard, courtesy Christine Verguson.

79

THE HUDDERSFIELD ELECTION

The nomination of candidates for the seat vacated by Mr Stansfield at Huddersfield, on the finding of a committee of the House of Commons that treating had been practised at the late election, took place at eleven o'clock on Wednesday morning. The hustings were erected in St George's Square and before them were assembled a crowd of many thousands of electors. The candidates were Viscount Goderich and Mr Joseph Starkey, the friends of the former being, generally speaking the supporters of Mr Willans, the defeated candidate at the late election, and those of the latter being the late supporters of Mr Stansfield, the unseated member. Both candidates profess to be Liberals, and the supporters of each having had experience to which bribery or treating may lead in the decision of the committees on the Hull and Huddersfield elections, adopted white favours as advocates of purity. On the left of the hustings, from the splendid stone warehouse of Messrs. Shaw, the white silk banner of one side floated, bearing the inscription – "Goderich for ever!" and from the handsome hotel on the opposite side of the square (the George) a similar white silk banner bore the cry of the other part, - "Starkey, our fellow-townsman!"

Manchester Guardian, 23 April 1853

REFORM MEETING AT HUDDERSFIELD

On Saturday afternoon, a large meeting of reformers was held in St George's-square, Huddersfield, under the auspices of the Reform League. The weather was very favourable for holding an open-air meeting, and a large number of persons came from the adjacent districts, accompanied by bands of music, of which thirteen entered the square, one of the most noticed being that from Sheepridge and Deighton, which was preceded by men bearing a large crimson banner on which was inscribed "Gladstone and Reform." The meeting was attended by some thousands of persons, and as the speakers could not make themselves heard at the outskirts of the crowd, a second meeting was held at the bottom of the square; the platform for the first meeting being placed beside the Russian cannons in the upper part of the square.

Leeds Mercury, 23 July 1866

POLITICS
AND PROTEST

BEFORE THE INTRODUCTION of the secret ballot in 1872, voting was a very public affair and bribery and 'treating' were commonplace. Following a petition from supporters of William Willans, the defeated candidate in the 1852 election, a parliamentary Select Committee on the Huddersfield Election Petition was convened in March 1853. A great deal of 'treating' appeared to have taken place in inns, beerhouses and the George Hotel and the Select Committee's decision that the result of the 1852 election was void meant that a new election was held on 23 April 1853. The *Huddersfield and Holmfirth Examiner* estimated that on polling day in 1853 there were around 20,000 in the Square when, it also calculated, only 1350 men were entitled to vote. Not only were there ladies at the windows of Shaw's warehouse waving white handkerchiefs but 'many hundreds if not thousands of women belonging to the humbler classes' were amongst the crowd. This was at a time when a minority of men and no women had the right to vote.

To an extent St George's Square can be said to reflect the history of democracy in this country. In 1866 thousands of working men and thirteen bands crowded into the Square in support of the Parliamentary Reform Bill which aimed to extend the franchise.

In a far from sympathetic report the Huddersfield *Chronicle* (28 July 1866) suggested that the crowd who had come to hear the speakers was outnumbered by 'idlers and onlookers'. It was estimated that between 18,000 and 20,000 people filled the Square on 11 October 1884 for a demonstration led by Liberal MPs in support of further extending the franchise. Here too were veterans who had supported the Great Reform Act of 1832, some of whom brought along their 'time-stained banners' including the Skelmanthorpe Flag, created in 1819 in response to the Peterloo Massacre. In 1926, weaver and historian Fred Lawton let the flag tell its own story:

My dear old master wishes me to write the story of my life, he thinks no one can do it so well as I can, and, as I lay neatly folded in my cosy drawer, I let my mind go back to the day of my birth, a day in October, 1819. So, I am 107 years old...

On the 11th October [1894], I again led the Skelmanthorpe Reformers to Huddersfield to a great franchise demonstration. The first meeting was held in St. George's Square. About 40,000 people were present. The speakers were W H Leatham, M.P., E A Leatham, M.P. and Charles Bradlaugh, M.P. They had put some large letters on my head which said I was a relic of the past. I was looked at with great interest as we marched through the crowded streets. My vanity was satisfied and I came home well pleased.

Fred Lawton, *Hirst Buckley's Annual*, 1926

Together with other places across the country, the Labour movement in Huddersfield held its first May Day in 1893 with a march ending in a rally in the Square calling for the eight hour day. It would be held every year in peacetime until 1997 and then revived in 2004 for a May Day march ahead of the European elections. There were certainly many thousands of people present at the 1906 May Day rally.

GREAT DAY IN HUDDERSFIELD

Large Labour meetings were held in Huddersfield yesterday. By St George's square during the afternoon, several thousands of people gathered to listen to the speakers. The Hippodrome was filled in the evening. Labour favours were conspicuous, the men wearing red ties. The women who formed a considerable proportion of the audience had adorned themselves with rosettes, and the children of the Socialist Sunday school wore red sashes.

The Lindley Brass Band accompanied the singing of Socialist songs. Mr Edgar Whiteley presided, and amongst the speakers at the afternoon meeting were Mr J.A. Seddon, MP (St Helens), Mr Victor Grayson (Manchester) and Mr T. Russell Williams (who has again been adopted as the prospective Labour and Socialist candidate for Huddersfield). The Chairman remarked that their Mayday meetings 'had been a splendid success and they would look back upon it as an epoch in the Labour movement in the town...'

Leeds Mercury, 7 May 1906

The Skelmanthorpe Flag,
now at the Tolson Museum,
courtesy Kirklees Image
Archive.

May Day Rally 1907,
courtesy Alan Brooke

The *Labour Leader*, a paper then edited by Keir Hardie, estimated that 25,000 people were in the Square to make Huddersfield's 1906 rally, given the size of the town, the most successful May Day rally ever to be held in England. Victor Grayson, who would be elected MP for Colne Valley in July 1907, was also present at the 1907 Rally as were Williams and Whitely and once again the *Labour Leader* reported that 25,000 people had filled the Square.

But it should be said that while they may not have been as well attended, reports in Huddersfield's socialist newspaper *The Worker* show that meetings frequently took place in the Square and often speakers would move between the Square and the Market Cross. In an interview in 1968, Arthur Gardiner (1889 – 1971) told Cyril Pearce how he first became interested in politics when, on one Sunday evening, he chanced upon a meeting in the Square. A Conscientious Objector in World War One, Arthur would later become a Huddersfield Councillor, Alderman, Mayor and Freeman of the Borough.

The first time I was drawn onto the fringe of the ranks of the socialist movement was a meeting I attended in St George's Square – an open-air meeting – which I thought was a fight or something going off in the Square when I saw this crowd – I ran up to see what was going on and there was a socialist meeting and Billy Gee of Northampton – I remember him today – was the speaker...

[Ramsay Macdonald] had a voice like an organ and he went on and on but when he'd finished, you'd say he'd made a marvellous speech but what he'd said, you couldn't tell anybody – all emotion. I remember his coming to address an outdoor meeting in St George's Square and he spoke from one of the George Hotel bedroom windows. The Square was packed. He was a very fine speaker.

ARTHUR GARDINER interviewed by CYRIL PEARCE 31 October 1968

Several meetings were held in the Square in support of women's suffrage – during the 1906 Huddersfield by-election large crowds gathered in the Square to hear Emmeline and Christabel Pankhurst and other speakers from the Women's Social and Political Union (WSPU), including eight women who came directly to Huddersfield, arriving at the railway station after their release from Holloway Prison. The by-election had provided the opportunity to oppose the Liberal government's candidate. The Liberals held on to the Huddersfield seat but historian Jill Liddington has pointed out that the activity around the by-election played a significant part in increasing awareness of the Votes for Women campaign in Huddersfield and in neighbouring communities. On 27 September 1908 a large crowd gathered in the Square (the WSPU paper, *Votes For Women*, estimated it to be between 20,000 and 50,000) to hear speeches from five speaker platforms arranged around the Peel statue. The speakers included Mrs Pankhurst, and her daughter Adela who had organised the rally. On the following evening Mrs Pankhurst spoke at the Parochial Hall where it was decided to open a literature stall every Saturday in the Square.

At all the platforms the following resolution was passed: - "This meeting calls upon the Government to enfranchise the women of the country on the same terms as men during the coming session of Parliament, and expresses admiration of the brave women who have suffered imprisonment for the cause of liberty."

Yorkshire Factory Times, 2 October 1908

Just a few days after the WSPU rally, 1000 people assembled in the Square to express what the *Yorkshire Factory Times* called 'Huddersfield's Workless Cry' (17 October 1908) and demand that the Borough Council find paid work for the jobless. In the 1920s, in the aftermath of the First World War, the unemployed would meet in the Square and then march to the Guardians' office to protest about the amount of relief. In September 1923 Arthur Brice, an unemployed engineer, wrote to the *Examiner* – the editor advised him to take up his complaints with the Clerk to the Guardians.

TO THE EDITOR

Sir, - Recently the Huddersfield unemployed marched to the Guardians' Office, in Ramsden Street, headed by the leaders, who were granted an interview with the authorities, at which interview it was arranged that the unemployed were either to be provided with work or something like a living grant. At the meeting held in St George's Square after the interview, the unemployed were informed that the authorities had offered 13s. each for man and wife, rents paid up to 15s. per week, with one bag of coal. These terms were put to a vote of the unemployed and accepted, with a strong protest. But, sir, small as this grant was, and willingly as (according to information received) the authorities had granted it, the unemployed are finding to their dismay that what the authorities agreed to is different altogether from what they do. Not half of the amount agreed to is being granted. Is it honest? Is it straightforward dealing? Is it the way to make starving desperate people honest when they see the real people's leaders so far from being honest? – Your, etc., ARTHUR BRICE

Huddersfield Daily Examiner, 7 May 1906

Conservatives also used the Square for political propaganda, sometimes in novel ways as when the Conservative Film Van visited the Square with a 'daylight exhibition' on the afternoon of Saturday 6 April 1929. The 'talkies' had arrived, and the Party could use the van to relay speeches to large crowds.

During the Second World War St George's Square was said to be unsuitable for large gatherings because of shelters and trolley buses but this was no longer an issue when people packed into the Square to see Winston Churchill during his whistle-top election tour on 26 June 1945. Churchill was an hour late in arriving and addressed the crowd for 30 minutes.

HUDDERSFIELD HECKLER

At Huddersfield a crowd of 40,000 packed St George's Square. "Big 'ner' a Cup-tie crowd" was the comment of one veteran. It was certainly the biggest election crowd seen in Huddersfield in living memory.

A cheer, which must have been heard a mile away, came from 40,000 throats as Mr Churchill ascended to the waggon which did duty as a platform, and was introduced by Mr J. D. Keaton.

As soon as Mr Churchill began to speak the good-humoured shouting ceased. There was just one heckler. When Mr Churchill remarked, "I feel we may say 'Trust the people and let the people trust us,'" a man in the crowd shouted, "We can't."

The Prime Minister paused, then continued: "That gentleman says you can't. That's all right. This is a free country, and everybody is entitled to express his opinion, but I am one up on him because I have the 'mike' and he hasn't."

There was a roar of laughter.

Yorkshire Observer, 27 June 1945.

Churchill's election visit to Huddersfield was not without controversy as the Mayor had planned to give Churchill a civic reception in the Square but this was opposed by the Liberal and Labour candidates who argued that he was in Huddersfield as leader of the Conservative Party, not as the wartime leader of the nation. Instead, the Mayor waited for him in St George's Street allowing the Prime Minister to lean out of his car, shake hands and sign the visitors' book.

The Hands Off HRI demo! A huge outpouring of feeling in support of our hospital.

ADRIAN LEE March 2022

Save Our A&E March (Huddersfield's biggest post-war march?)

KATIE May 2022

Today probably the most remembered demonstrations in the Square are those that took place in 2016 to save Huddersfield Royal Infirmary's Accident and Emergency department – on 23 January around 1000 people were in the Square to protest against the closure and a month later, on 27 February, up to 8000 people took part in what was described as the biggest turnout since the Second World War.

ABOVE RIGHT
'Hands Off HRI' rally, 23 January 2016, courtesy John Lambe.

RIGHT
Enough is Enough rally, 1 October 2022, courtesy Beverley Norris.

There has only been enough space to describe just a few of the rallies and protests that have taken place in the Square over the years and the different causes that have brought people there to stand alongside their fellow citizens. Beverley was in St George's Square on 1 October 2022 for just one of the many protests taking place across the country as part of the Enough is Enough movement, formed in response to the cost-of-living crisis. This led her to reflect on some of the reasons people had to be there.

Politics and protest continue to bring people into the Square.

The buildings around St George's Square are evidence of the wealth created by Huddersfield people over the centuries. Being in the Square for the Enough is Enough rally on the 1st of October 2022 made me think of the ongoing struggle working people have had to obtain a decent standard of living, despite their contribution. All types of essential workers, who had been applauded on a weekly basis for their heroic efforts during the pandemic, have since found themselves having to fight against real wage cuts and attacks upon the services they provide. It was a good feeling to stand alongside fellow healthcare, rail, council, postal, civil service, and education workers. A feeling of the power of solidarity was being kindled in the sunshine of the Square that day.

BEVERLEY NORRIS August 2023

PATRIOTISM AND ROYALTY

George Hotel with one of two trophy Sebastopol cannon that were on display in the Square 1858-1873, courtesy Christopher R Marsden.

HUDDERSFIELD PEOPLE GATHERED in St George's Square to express their patriotism. Although the Crimean War had ended in April 1856, 29 May was the day set aside across the country for national rejoicing. The enthusiasm with which Huddersfield embraced the day was particularly noted by the *Manchester Guardian*, the town 'being entirely given up to pleasure'. The *Huddersfield Chronicle* described the events of the day and those present at greater length, remarking that the singing was such that it could be heard as far away as Lindley and Crosland Moor. The *Examiner* report was more restrained, remarking that the size of the procession had 'never been equalled in this neighbourhood' and that it was good to see that people were coming together and making the most of the holiday.

HUDDERSFIELD
(From our Correspondent by Electric Telegraph)

THURSDAY NIGHT. – Today, the town of Huddersfield was entirely given up to pleasure, all the shops being shut, and business suspended. In accordance with a programme, the procession left St George's Square a little after twelve o'clock, pacing along John William-street, Kirkgate, and all the principal streets, and being finally arranged in the following order:- The C troop of Yeomanry, headed by their band, with drums and fifes; Crimean soldiers and pensioners in a waggon, with a trophy and Russian arms, ornamented with evergreens; the clergy in their gowns, ministers of various denominations, magistrates, improvement commissioners, waterworks commissioners, gentlemen and tradesmen; the freemasons, headed by the Bramley brass band; a great number of secret orders and benevolent societies, from the town and district, with emblematic banners and appropriate devices and mottoes; various Sunday schools, of all denominations, from Huddersfield and the district, numbering about 15,000 children and teachers, in four divisions, with an immense number of flags and banners, beautifully decorated with appropriate devices. The procession extended several miles in length and occupied an hour and a half in passing. At half-past four p.m. all had arrived, and taken the position assigned to them in St George's Square. A selection of sacred music, including Handel's "Hallelujah Chorus" and concluding with the national anthem was then performed with great effect by 520 musicians and vocalists, who were stationed upon an elevated platform in front of the railway station. The assemblage was estimated to amount to from 35,000 to 40,000 persons, including Sunday school scholars; and the coup d'oeil throughout the proceedings was novel and interesting. The proceedings closed with an immense round of cheering, about five p.m. when the vast assemblage began to disperse.

Manchester Guardian, 30 May 1856.

On 19 May 1900 a large crowd also gathered in the Square to celebrate the Relief of Mafeking. The 217-day siege of the town (now called Mafikeng) during the Second Boer War had been lifted just two days earlier. This was followed up a week later by an editorial in the *Huddersfield Chronicle* (26 May 1900), suggesting that the meeting in the Square was very different to the usual Saturday 'parade' and critical of the town leaders for failing to provide 'official guidance' regarding the celebrations.

THE MEETING IN ST GEORGE'S SQUARE

On Saturday morning, when the weather is fine, there is always a parade of fashion along John William Street and New Street, but on Saturday it was gayer than usual. Everybody appeared at his or her best, and all the colours of the rainbow were seen. Many of the townspeople wore emblems of one kind or another. The most popular was the Baden-Powell button; another one was a red, white and blue rosette with button suspended; and lilies of the valley, bound with white ribbon, were largely worn; and ordinary red, white and blue favours were very general. Very little children were seen carrying flags. Troops of children in khaki marched around the streets singing patriotic songs, and members of the Army Veterans' Association moved around the crowded streets. Even dogs and horses were decorated with red, white and blue ribbons. The tram engines and the railway parcel vans carried their flags, mostly Union Jacks; cyclists decked their machines with favours; and the whipstocks of "cabbies" were banded with red, white and blue...

Huddersfield Daily Examiner,
21 May 1900

Royal events have also brought people into the Square, even when no visit has been involved. The marriage of Edward, Prince of Wales, to Princess Alexandra of Denmark in March 1863 was such a day and Huddersfield had plans for lighting up the Square. Rain cut short the afternoon celebrations, but not before a balloon ascent had taken place in the Square! Later in the day thousands congregated in the Square to witness the spectacle of a firework display funded by public subscription.

THE MARRIAGE OF THE PRINCE OF WALES PREPARATIONS IN HUDDERSFIELD

The most general activity now prevails in the work of decoration and illumination, and the town bids fair to wear a becoming air of rejoicing and brilliancy on the occasion of the happy event to be consummated during the ensuing week. The elegant piles of buildings which constitute the pride of the town, situate in St George's-Square, John William-street, and the locality, have during the past week been the scene of busy operations on the part of plumbers, gas fitters, &c. The handsome portico front of the Railway Station will be outlined by gas which promises to be very effective. A serpentine wreath of jets will encircle the large Corinthian pillars at either end, and brilliant devices will be exhibited in the centre. The entrances to the booking offices will also be brilliant with gas jets and devices. Britannia Buildings, the George Hotel, the Lion Arcade, and most of the warehouses in the Square, will also be illuminated in a style worthy of their noble proportions...

Huddersfield Chronicle, 7 March 1863

Queen Victoria Diamond Jubilee celebrations, courtesy Kirklees Image Archive

Queen Victoria's Diamond Jubilee was, declared the *Huddersfield Daily Examiner*, celebrated in the town 'in such a way that those who took part in it are likely not to forget it their lives long'.

THE SCENE IN THE SQUARE

Arrived in St George's Square, the sight was probably the greatest and most impressive ever witnessed there. The Square proper - that part laid with sets – was nearly filled with Sunday scholars and teachers, and week-day scholars, the latter of whom not connected with Sunday schools had joined Sunday scholars who assembled nearest to the respective elementary schools. Some of the scholars got blocked in Northumberland Street and streets nearby, and had been unable to move forward for nearly three-quarters of an hour. They, however, got into the Square very soon after the arrival of the head of the procession there, and found their way within the strong barriers on each side of the roadway left in the middle of the Square... The total estimated was upwards of 17,000; but most of the Sunday schools exceeded their estimate by the addition of day scholars not connected with them, and probably by a good number of adults, becoming scholars for the occasion.

...In addition to the 18,368 children penned in by the barriers there were immense numbers of people on the pavements each side of the Square, all along John William Street extending beyond the Square at each end, in Northumberland Street, on the railway companies' ground in front of the railway station and in Railway and Station Streets, only sufficient space being kept clear to enable passengers to get to and from the station. It was a truly magnificent concourse of well-ordered people; scholars, teachers, processionists, and spectators could not have numbered fewer than 50,000 persons, and the children's straw hats and many head trimmings, and the varied colours of adult ladies' adornments, together with the uniforms of the Yeomanry and Volunteers, made up an almost bewilderingly bright mass in the brilliant sunshine. The scene was rendered more animated by the fact that at the windows and on the roofs and parapets of the railway station, the George Hotel, and warehouses and offices commanding a view of the Square and its approaches were hundreds of persons of all ages, most of those at the windows being ladies in gay attire...

Huddersfield Daily Examiner, 23 June 1897.

Procession of the Duke of Somerset passing Estate Buildings, 7 June 1883, courtesy Kirklees Local Studies Library

It should be said that a very similar celebration had taken place two days earlier – a Sunday – with an estimated 20,000 Sunday school pupils and their teachers assembling in the Square.

The first royal visit to Huddersfield was made on 13 October 1883 when the Duke and Duchess of Albany came to formally open Beaumont Park and to visit the Fine Art and Industrial Exhibition at Huddersfield Technical College's Ramsden Building. At 10.45am the royal couple - the Duke of Albany was Prince Leopold, Queen Victoria's fourth son - arrived at Huddersfield Railway Station and, on arrival, they were received in the First-Class Refreshment Room and addressed by the Mayor and members of the Borough Council. A detachment of the Second Volunteer Battalion, West Riding Regiment, provided the Guard of Honour. Three pages in the official programme are devoted to 'police arrangements': 165 police officers were to be drafted in from neighbouring towns and Huddersfield's own mounted police were to be at the railway station at 9.15am. The visit passed without incident with the Duke and Duchess arriving back in St George's Square at 5pm to catch their train. When, earlier in the year, the Duke of Somerset came to Huddersfield to open both the Exhibition and the new Ramsden Building, Estate Buildings – decorated in patriotic regalia – provided spectators with an excellent vantage point to see him pass by in an open carriage.

The Revell sisters had an equally good vantage point when Princess Margaret came to Huddersfield in 1958 to open Huddersfield High School for Girls (now Salendine Nook High School) and her visit also made an impression on a young Adrian Lee which he was to recall later during his time at Huddersfield New College.

RIGHT
A royal walkabout: Queen Elizabeth in the Square 2007, courtesy Mark Hemingway Photography.

Mum took me, pre-school age in the late 1950s, to the top of Northumberland Street for the arrival of Princess Margaret. I have the memory of a "big car" turning out of the Square into John William Street – headed for the Salendine Nook campus of three new schools. Whilst I was there, Huddersfield New College's Princess Margaret Cup always reminded me of that day.

ADRIAN LEE, March 2022

Our father had an accountancy practice at 7 St George's Square, Revell and Revell. When Princess Margaret visited Huddersfield, we stood on the desk in the general office and from the window watched her car go round the Square amidst the crowds

SYLVIA ARNOLD & ALISON REVELL,
December 2021

Thursday 24 May, 2007 - the sun poured down on St George's Square, and on the many people who had taken their place in the Square several hours before the Royal couple were due to arrive. The Queen and the Duke of Edinburgh had come to the Square to enjoy a very special preview from Huddersfield Choral Society and Opera North of the People's Prom Concert to be performed there in the evening. Before they took their seats amongst the VIPs, they found time for a quick walkabout amongst the people behind the barriers. The Queen then went onto the stage to have a few words with the choir and orchestra. The concert ended with a rousing rendition of the Dambusters theme as the Queen and Prince Philip were departing.

HM the Queen and the Duke of Edinburgh came to town in May 2007. Lunch (a curry) at the University — and by pure fluke when I was heading to the Shorehead roundabout the Police outriders and the Royal car passed very closely by on the other carriageway headed for their University function prior to afternoon commitments. I was due to see them in the Square in the afternoon as I had an invitation to the VIP area where the Royal couple were to be seated for entertainment from the Huddersfield Choral Society and the Orchestra of Opera North. Following that they very cleverly entered the station at "The George" end only to appear at the opposite end of the station and then head on to the stage to meet the performers. They left the Square to go to Crosland Hill airfield to fly by helicopter to Scotland for a meeting with the then First Minister. An interesting journey for the Royal couple through Thornton Lodge and Crosland Moor! That evening there was an outstanding concert with the same musical forces ending with a spectacular firework display.

ADRIAN LEE, March 2022

I was fortunate in being invited to the marquee for the visit of the Queen and Duke of Edinburgh. I was among a small group on the raised podium from which the Queen would address the crowd, gathered in the square. Unfortunately, I stood behind some taller people and the Queen, being rather small, passed in front, leaving me with only the sight of her hat bobbing up and down across the stage. My only memory of the occasion is her hat, though I forget its colour.

DAVID WYLES, December 2021

In 2007 the Square came to life, buzzing with excitement. Queen Elizabeth II and Prince Phillip arrived, following a visit to the university, to listen to the concert set up in the Square and receive flowers. The music and merriment continued after they left

MICHELLE KAIN, October 2022

We'll Be Good Boys

It's bonfire day on Thursday,
And Willie Jones and me,
Have made our minds to obey,
Those little bills we see
Put up by order of the chief
Police authority.

We will not light our bonfire
Within St George's Square,
For fear a wicked Zeppelin
Is prowling in the air,
For it would show the Germans that
The Railway Station's there.

From a verse by FROTH,
Huddersfield Daily Examiner, 3 November 1914

WAR AND PEACE

THE ROLE St George's Square played in the town in times of war and its use by the military did not begin in 1914. We have already seen how crowds gathered in the Square to celebrate the end of the Crimean War and the lifting of the siege at Mafeking, but it had long provided a space suitable for military displays. In 1855 a visit from a company of Dragoon Guards, believed to be en route to the Crimea, brought many spectators out into the Square.

MILITARY EXCITEMENT, - It is not often that the peaceable inhabitants of Huddersfield are drawn from their usual business pursuits to witness the imposing spectacle of a troop of a British cavalry passing through the town. On Wednesday evening and Thursday morning, however, the whole town was in a state of great excitement consequent on the temporary visit of a company of the 1st Dragoon Guards en route from Leeds to Liverpool...On Thursday morning the whole company assembled in St George's Square, accompanied by the band of the Yeomanry, who played several national and popular airs, the chorus of which was heard by upwards of 3000 people, who had assembled to witness their departure. About half-past eight o'clock they prepared to leave, and on proceeding from the square and along the entire route to the utmost limits of the town, they were warmly cheered by the immense mass of people assembled, to which they heartily responded. They left Huddersfield by the romantic road of Blackstone for Rochdale. We believe their ultimate destination is the seat of war in the Crimea.

Leeds Intelligencer, 28 July 1855

While over the years many regular army units passed through the Square, the various volunteer forces formed in and around Huddersfield regularly paraded there and many of the businessmen who owned premises in the Square served as officers. The march past in the Square on 1 June 1864 by the Huddersfield Troop of 2nd West Yorkshire Yeomanry Cavalry reflected the usual pattern of these events – after the march past had been dismissed, luncheon was provided at the George by Sergeant-Major Wigney, who was also the proprietor of the hotel.

The Huddersfield Rifle Club, the direct ancestor of the Territorial Army in Huddersfield, was constituted on 22 June 1859 following a 'meeting of gentlemen'. Part of a county-wide, indeed national, movement, the Huddersfield Rifle Corps was soon officially designated the 10th West Riding of Yorkshire Volunteers and after a further meeting at the George Hotel, a drill instructor was employed, and a black uniform adopted. Following the reorganisation of the Army's infantry regiments (the Childers Reforms) in 1881, the Huddersfield corps became the 2nd (Volunteer) Battalion of the Duke of Wellington's West Riding Regiment. But it was not only Volunteers from Huddersfield who drilled in the Square – the Saddleworth Volunteers were there in 1895 after their drill instructor had committed suicide.

> ...rightly or wrongly, the men looked upon the unfortunate act as being due to what they called "browbeating" by the adjutant. It is characteristic of Saddleworth folks that when they have a grievance on their minds they let it out to the full. At a parade, held shortly after, in St. George's Square, Huddersfield, they went for the adjutant in old Saddleworth fashion and hooted him to their hearts content, a breach of discipline which led the military authorities to disband the company.
>
> Aaron Wrigley, *The Wind Among the Heather*, Huddersfield, 1916 p.244

Many of the Huddersfield Volunteers responded to the call and served in the South African War – those who were lost are remembered on the memorial in Greenhead Park. Further army reforms in 1908 led to the creation of the Territorial Force and the division of the Huddersfield Battalion into the 5th Battalion (Huddersfield) and the 7th Battalion (Colne Valley). On the eve of the country entering World War One on the 4 August 1914 both battalions were recalled from their annual camp at Marske in North Yorkshire with crowds gathering outside the station to await their return. On the morning of Wednesday, 5 August, 450 men and officers from the 5th marched from

5th Battalion, West Riding Regiment, the Dukes, arriving at the station, 5 September 1914.

Huddersfield Drill Hall to the station where they were drawn up into lines. The *Examiner* reported that while there was a large crowd in the Square, there was 'no marked demonstration' with some of the men singing and shouting 'Are we downhearted?' as they marched into the station. Six hundred men from the Colne Valley battalion were, meanwhile, waiting on the station's island platform.

It is not surprising that activities and displays aimed at recruitment took place in the Square. In April 1915 Harry Lauder's Pipe Band paid the town a visit – Lauder, the most popular musical hall entertainer of the day, had formed the band to help the recruitment drive. As well as appearing at Victoria Hall in the evenings, on the first day ex-soldiers in the band assembled in the Square for a route march to Almondbury, and back, while on the third afternoon Lauder's band took part in a recruitment meeting. And on 8 May 1915 a 'great military display' in the Square, organised by the Huddersfield Recruitment Committee, was even captured on film!

On Saturday last, a great military display was held in Huddersfield. Over 6,000 troops were marched into the town from four different points, and a grand march past was held, with St George's Square as the saluting base. The management of the Empire secured a remarkable film of the proceedings, and their enterprise was rewarded by packed houses at each performance.

Kinematograph Weekly, 20 May 1915

In September a 'Flying Column' of the West Riding Regiment (Territorials) held a short recruitment meeting in the Square as did the West Riding Divisional Cyclist Company in October. In addition to the Recruitment Office at the Drill Hall, there were local recruiting offices in Railway Street and in the Square itself where, according to the *Examiner* in December 1915, the staff were extremely busy.

But vehicles were also required to help the war effort. Just a few days after the war began on 12 August 1914, E. Gordon Learoyd, a solicitor with an office in Lion Chambers, placed a notice in the local press, asking motorcar owners who were willing to lend their vehicles to the War Office to get in touch with him. The Huddersfield Automobile Club noted in January 1915 that hardly a day passed without their members being asked to lend their cars for conveying the wounded to hospitals, Belgian refugees from place to place and other war-related activities. In April the Club – Learoyd was its secretary at the time – took the decision to form a local platoon of the National Motor Transport Volunteers (NMV). In Huddersfield they would play a major role in collecting convoys of wounded soldiers from the station and transporting them to the war hospitals in the area. They also provided a 'rest room' in the Square – this was visited in just one week in February 1917 by 206 wounded soldiers.

While the Square was the logical place to hold large recruitment meetings, it was also – with its long association with political meetings – the place where people gathered to express opposition to the war.

Huddersfield Motor Transport Section (Volunteers) on parade - they provided their own transport.

HUDDERSFIELD AND THE WAR LOCAL LABOUR FEELING
Strong protest at Mass Meetings

At the great meeting in St George's Square, Huddersfield, on Sunday night references were made to the then impending calamity of war, and the following resolution was carried at both platforms:
"That this meeting of citizens of Huddersfield views with horror the acts of war in which European nations have already engaged, and which threaten to involve the whole continent of Europe in an orgy of bloodshed unparalleled in the history of mankind. We protest in the strongest possible terms against this country being embroiled in the insane conflict, and call upon Parliament to refuse sanction to any measures in that direction.
"That this resolution be forwarded to the Speaker of the House of Commons, the Prime Minister, Mr A. J. Sherwell MP and the chairman of the Labour Party..."

The Worker, 8 August 1914

This is just the beginning of a long report in Huddersfield's socialist weekly newspaper, *The Worker*, on two meetings (one in the afternoon and one in the evening) held in the Square on the Sunday immediately before Britain entered the war. The evening meeting took place using two platforms and Jess Townend, secretary of the Huddersfield branch of the Workers Union, in moving the resolution remarked that 'All the kings interested were praying to God to help them come out victorious. What a pickle God must be in.'

The history and extent of Huddersfield's opposition to the war has been told by Cyril Pearce in his ground-breaking study of the district's conscientious objectors, *Comrades in Conscience* (2001). The Military Service Act (No 2) came into operation on 10 February 1916. *The Worker*'s reporter was in the Square in May to see Joseph Flanders publicly burn his call-up papers.

A CONSCRIPT'S DRAMATIC ACT

After the meeting had concluded and the speakers had left the platform, Mr Joseph A. Flanders and Mr H. B. Flanders mounted the wagon. The former, producing his calling-up notice, said that for many years he had been a Socialist and an anti-militarist, and he was there to make a protest against being called up under the Military Service Act. He added: "As a proof I openly and solemnly swear that I will not serve under any military law or do any service likely to assist any military organisation. As further proof I will publicly burn the papers the military authorities have given me."
The calling-up paper was then burned. Mr H. B. Flanders called for three cheers "for a man who has the courage of his convictions." The audience responded, and also sang "The Red Flag."

The Worker, 6 May 1916

Ambulance trains with specially adapted carriages were used to bring casualties back from the front line. Huddersfield set a record in November 1917, in comparison with all the other towns the train had visited and even its own earlier record, when 7032 people passed through a train, newly fitted out by the Lancashire and Yorkshire Railway. Admission was by ticket only (1s.) and the money raised was to go towards 'extra comforts' for the wounded. The queue to view the ambulance train wound round the Square.

Huddersfield looked upwards in February 1918 to witness a daring aerial display over the Square.

...A brilliant exhibition of airmanship was given by two airmen who visited Huddersfield yesterday. One of the machines which flew over Huddersfield at about half-past four made some particularly daring manoeuvres in St George's Square. The machine first crossed the town east of the Square, "looping the loop" then came round with a quick turn, ascended for the moment over the station, and swooped down quickly towards the Square.

It seemed almost as if the skids of the machine must get entangled with the tramway wires, and so low was it that the distinguishing marks of the machine could be very plainly seen. Passing over the concert platform the pilot dropped a number of leaflets – a good shot, if he intended them, as one supposed, to fall into the very heart of the crowd. That manoeuvre was again repeated, and the aeroplane then soared away. It was an exhilarating moment for those in the Square as the machine swooped down upon them, and the two youngest of our arms – the Tank and the aeroplane made a very odd contrast.

There was little business done in the shops and business houses near the Square and in the town yesterday afternoon...

Huddersfield Daily Examiner, 19 February 1918.

The air display had coincided with Tank Days when people were encouraged to visit the Square to throw money into the war-savings tank on display there. Schoolchildren were even given a half-day's holiday on 21 February so they could march to the Square, accompanied by their teachers, and make their own small contributions to the war-effort.

Even before the war came to an end, there were those in the town who were already anticipating some of the problems that would need to be faced when peace came. In September 1917 a Huddersfield branch of the National Association of Discharged Sailors and Soldiers had been formed and a 'mass meeting' was held in the Square to highlight the plight of the disabled as well as those who would not be able to live on their pensions, including widows and other dependents of soldiers killed in action.

Armistice Day, Monday 11 November 1918, was not greeted with any sort of official celebration. At the annual Mayor-making ceremony which had taken place two days earlier, the way the town should mark the firing of the 'Last Shot' was discussed. Alderman Wheatley said, 'The best suggestion was for the mills to close, and the people to gather in the Square as one happy family. They had held meetings there to get the army together and to get their money. Surely, they could gather there at that happy moment'. Alderman Woodhead replied that in wintertime the proper place for such a gathering should be in the Town Hall. It was finally agreed that every place of worship should be asked to hold a service, twenty-four hours after the signing of the armistice.

Throughout the 1920s and 1930s people gathered in the Square to observe the two-minute silence on Armistice Day. In 1928 it was estimated that there were between five and six thousand people in the Square with a similar number gathering at the War Memorial in Greenhead Park, where a wireless relay of the Cenotaph Service from London could be heard. It is not surprising that the railwaymen, employed by what was by then the LMS, usually observed the two-minute silence in the Square.

Standing on railway drays outside Huddersfield station members of the Huddersfield L.M.S. Band, in their working clothes, accompanied the singing of hymns at the service in St George's Square, attended by 3,000 people. Prayers were said from the station steps by the Rev. W. R. Chignall, curate of the Parish Church. The crowd in the square was not so large as usual. Huddersfield's principal service was held in Greenhead Park...

Yorkshire Evening Post, 11 November 1936

Although the main Armistice Day services had moved to the War Memorial, in 1937 a maroon was fired from the Corporation Tramways Office (then on the corner with Northumberland Street) to mark the beginning of the silence and a second fired at the end of the two minutes.

As it had in the Great War, in the Second World War the Square provided a convenient space to raise funds - and indeed morale - to support the war effort, with a series of local war savings weeks. During Huddersfield War Weapons Week in November 1940 a 'giant German bomber', a naval gun on an armoured waggon and 'various types of bombs' were put on display with collecting sheets placed near the exhibits. A pavilion was erected to act as a 'selling centre bureau'. The money raised from contributions across the district and from businesses as well as individuals soon exceeded the Huddersfield Savings Committee's original target. Huddersfield and its surrounding district raised £2,351,329 in total during the 1940 War Weapons week, of which £994 10s 7d was raised through the collection sheets placed next to the German bomber in the Square. This would go towards providing destroyers for the navy.

Other savings campaign weeks followed – during Huddersfield Warship Week in March 1942 gramophone records were played repetitively out of several loudspeakers around the Square. In May 1944 a salvo was fired in the Square when the district exceeded its target of £1,250,000 during Salute the Soldier week.

Tanks reappeared in the Square in August 1941 when the Royal Armoured Corps, who had fought in France and Libya, brought a Matilda and two Valentine tanks into the Square as part of a Speed the Tanks campaign. But perhaps one of the most surprising events in landlocked Huddersfield was the presentation of a boat to the Huddersfield Sea Cadet Corps in September 1943. A notice placed in the *Examiner* claimed that this was the first time a 'naval auxiliary' had been launched on dry land outside a railway station!

At 9.30am on 8 May 1945 an illuminated trolley bus, decked out with bunting, fairy lights and huge Vs on its side, left St George's Square on a tour of the district, but it was not in the Square itself but outside the Town Hall that Huddersfield people gathered to hear Huddersfield's mayor, Alderman Sidney Kaye, mark the end of the war in Europe.

Printed programme for the presentation of a boat to the Sea Cadets, 25 September 1943, courtesy WYAS Kirklees.

...Speaking in St George's Square today, Mr Vic Oliver, who is appearing at a Huddersfield theatre, said: "Tomorrow is the birthday of my dear father-in-law, Mr Winston Churchill. I shall be seeing him on Sunday, and it would make a great birthday present if I could say that I just returned from Huddersfield where they had passed every other city so far as War Weapons Week is concerned."

Yorkshire Post,
30 November 1940

No. 1038

Sea Cadet Corps
Huddersfield ("Nelson") Unit
(Commanding Officer, Lieut. W. E. Burnett, R.N.V.R.)

PROGRAMME

Ceremony of Presentation of Boat

INSPECTION
by
Admiral J. G. P. Vivian, C.B.
(Admiral Commanding Reserves)

in St. George's Square

Saturday, 25th September, 1943 at 2·45 p.m.

Fireplaces and Cooking Ranges	The best Selection can be made at the Showrooms of John Mollett Ltd. John William Street, Phone 4343/4 Huddersfield

FAITH IN
THE SQUARE

THE BAND OF HOPE, a temperance organisation for children, was founded in Leeds in 1847. Members were taught the 'evils of drink' and took a pledge of total abstinence. It is difficult to overestimate how many children at this

THE UNITED BAND OF HOPE DEMONSTRATION THE PROCESSION

Ominous as the clouds looked during this morning, especially when, shortly before noon, a shower of rain fell, the weather has kept fine and bright since, and out of seventy-eight bands of hope that promised to take part in the procession at the united demonstration of the Huddersfield Band of Hope Union and the Huddersfield Church of England Temperance Society, no fewer than seventy-seven – a far larger number than on any former occasion – assembled in St George's Square. To see them start off their parade, as great crowds of holiday folks as ever made their way to the Square and the streets converging upon it, and gave the detachment of police (who went to the Square rather late), under the direction of the Chief Constable (Mr Ward), plenty of work to do to keep the space clear for the processionists to move out of the Square without breaking rank. Yet this was managed most successfully, although there were so many bands of hope, with their horses and waggons, and the procession numbered about 15,000 exclusive of brass bands. Windows of warehouses looking upon St. George's Square and the windows of the George Hotel were filled by persons who sought to view the procession under the most comfortable conditions. The various bands of hope made their way to their appointed places, with flags flying, and banners breasting the breeze, in a perfectly orderly manner, while the music of a variety of quicksteps, played by many brass bands, was heard coming from all points in rivalling cadences and inspiriting strains.

Huddersfield Daily Examiner, 23 May 1893

time were involved in Band of Hope activities on a weekly basis, but the Whitsuntide parade was always the highlight of the year. The *Examiner* reporter went on to say that 'no Whitsuntide procession was ever better assembled on its way than was this one – the greatest of the lot', and, as it happened, a cameraman was also present. The newspaper report failed to mention the onlookers perched, somewhat less comfortably, on the railway station roof!

The *Huddersfield Chronicle* estimated that between 35,000 and 40,000 people must have taken part in the demonstration when it arrived at Greenhead Park, suggesting that this may have not been as many as attended the previous year. A photo taken by optician and watchmaker Lewis Cousens around 1912 clearly shows how the children from Mount Pleasant Wesleyan Chapel dressed for the occasion – these girls may even have taken part in the maypole dancing that took place in the Square before the procession set off for Greenhead Park, where various sport contests and other activities awaited.

Whit Tuesday, 23 May 1893 - Huddersfield and District Band of Hope Union and Church of England Band of Hope Section grand procession setting off to Greenhead Park for the 24th annual demonstration, courtesy Christopher R Marsden.

While the Band of Hope Whitsuntide celebration usually took place on Whit Tuesday, Huddersfield's Catholic community favoured the holiday Monday for their Whitsuntide procession. As the *Examiner* reported in 1936, the annual Catholic procession was the oldest in the town. Although it was nowhere near as large as the Band of Hope processions, by the 1930s, with three parishes joining together it was attracting several thousand people. A May Queen always accompanied the procession – in 1936 St Patrick's May Queen was Netta Ganon and St Joseph's was Winifred Kaye.

In 1969 the Huddersfield Sikh community marked the 500th birthday of Guru Nunak with a procession which went through St George's Square on 23 November 1969, when it was photographed (overleaf) by Evald Sotnik, a member of the Huddersfield Borough Transport Department Photographic Club.

Band of Hope Whitsuntide demonstration c 1912 photographed by Lewis Cousens, courtesy Christopher R. Marsden.

MANY THOUSANDS IN A SPECTACULAR WALK

...Those taking part assembled in St George's Square, which was thronged with spectators, and in the bursts of sunshine a brilliant spectacle was seen. The hymn, "Faith of Our Fathers," was sung, and the procession moved on its way through Northumberland Street, Byram Street, Cross Church Street, Ramsden Street and New Street to the churches where Benediction was given. The usual children's treats were afterwards held...

The procession was headed by the Papal Standard of yellow and white, with the tiara and Keys of Peter, and by the Denaby Silver Prize Band. Some of the children carried bannerettes – among them the Holy Child of Prague and Our Lady of Perpetual Succour. All were beautifully dressed, and the boys looked very smart in their uniform of grey, green and yellow.

...The Children of Mary were a striking feature in their blue and white gowns, and the little children – many in white, but some in dresses of bright colours – offered a refreshing note...

Huddersfield Daily Examiner, 1 June 1936

500th birthday of Guru Nunak, courtesy Christopher R. Marsden,
Sotnik-Dixon collection.

SPORT AND THE SQUARE

IN 1922 HUDDERSFIELD Town won the FA Cup but this was not the first or last time they have been celebrated in the Square. In the 1920s, under the management of Herbert Chapman, they were the best team in England. Not only were they league champions for three successive seasons, but they also appeared in four FA Cup Finals.

A GREAT DEMONSTRATION

A very remarkable demonstration was witnessed in Huddersfield when the victorious Town team returned with the Association Cup. The winners arrived in Huddersfield about half-past-two by the Grand Central express from Marylebone and found awaiting them a very pleased and excited crowd which has been estimated at from 25,000 to 30,000 people.

Barriers had been erected in St George's Square, outside the station in anticipation of a crush, but the crowd exceeded all anticipations. It overflowed from the Square into John William Street, which was lined 12 deep on either side, and into New Street and it packed Ramsden Street in front of the Town Hall. The engine which drew the train into Huddersfield was decorated with the team's blue and white colours, and as it emerged from the tunnel it exploded a noisy salvo of fog signals.

The Deputy Mayor (Alderman Woolven) in the absence of the Mayor received the team. Motor-cars, all decorated with the Town colours, and bearing legends of welcome were waiting for the team and as they drove through the principal streets to the Town Hall, the band struck up 'See the Conquering Hero Comes'. Every window in St George's Square, John William Street, Market Place, New Street and Ramsden Street was crowded with faces. Every tram car, motor car or other vehicle which could be repositioned in John William Street was crowded with supporters and photographers. As the motor car conveying the players moved along the street, Wilson held the cup aloft and was greeted with rounds and rounds of cheering...

Yorkshire Post and Leeds Intelligencer, 2 May 1922

> When Huddersfield Town FC were promoted to the Premier League in 2017 and we all gathered for the parade in St George's Square.
>
> DANIELLE, October 2022

Many Town fans will share Danielle's memory of gathering in St George's Square to celebrate the success of the team in 2017. Some would have got tickets and been at the deciding match at Wembley when Huddersfield beat Reading after a nail-biting penalty shoot-out. No tickets were required however for the celebrations in St George's Square and fans turned out in their thousands.

There are some people in the town who prefer to support the teams of neighbouring places. Richard is certainly not one of them, but he has confessed to asking players from one such team for their autographs in the Square.

Crowd celebrating Town's promotion to the Premiership 2017, photographed by Huddersfield Town AFC photographer, John Early.

What a day in the history of St George's Square! Town against all the odds had gained promotion to the Premier League. The team with a meagre budget had amazed the pundits. We believed and yes there we were massed in our thousands, shoulder to shoulder. The triumphal open top bus, the jubilant Terrier team, manager Wagner and owner Dean Hoyle came into view amidst the deafening chants and cheers. The trophy was visible for us all to see.

The atmosphere was electric; a blue and white army, chanting, cheering, celebrating, welcoming our heroes back to a Northern town – the birthplace of Harold Wilson, whose statue draped in Town colours looked on in the midst of the square. There was a sea of blue and white; children on parents' shoulders, fans adorned with scarves waving flags and with the proud stone lion on Lion Chambers draped in a blue and white scarf. Even the rain later didn't dampen our enthusiasm. It was a day that will go down in the history of the Square and one I certainly will never forget.

SHARON KELLY, August 2021

I can't believe I'm admitting to this but I once asked four Leeds United players for their autographs! In my defence it was before they became known as "Dirty Leeds", but still! Checking Terry Frost's "Huddersfield Town: A Complete Record 1910-1990" the date must have been October 12th 1963 and Town lost 2-0. The players – Johnny Giles, Ian Lawson, Bobby Collins and Grenville Hair – were walking around St. George's Square at the same time as we, schoolboys, got off the Baddeley's coach that had taken us to a Saturday morning sports fixture at somewhere like Heckmondwike or Hipperholme. I assume they'd been in a team meeting at the Hotel and were killing time before moving off to Leeds Road.

Later, that dinnertime amateur sportsmen would be meeting in front of the Bank ready to go to their afternoon matches. It was rumoured that anyone wanting a game could go round asking if any team was short of a player.

RICHARD HOBSON, November 2021

In a world before smartphones, or even Ceefax, Bill remembers how his father used the Square to make sure he was up to date with the all the sports results.

Subject to memory fallibility! My father stopped his car on a corner (Lion Buildings?) in the mid 1950s to buy the sporting results newspapers – pink, green (and yellow?) on a Saturday evening.

BILL JAGGER, September 2021

Following the meeting at the George Hotel which led to the birth of Rugby League in 1895, the Huddersfield team, playing at the Fartown ground, had considerable success. In 1909 St George's Square was the scene of the celebrations for their victory in the Yorkshire Northern Union Cup on a scale which even attracted the attention of the national press.

FOOTBALL FRENZY REMARKABLE SCENES AT HUDDERSFIELD

On returning home last night from Leeds, where they defeated Batley in the final round of the Yorkshire Northern Union Cup, the Huddersfield team were accorded a reception which for wild enthusiasm is unprecedented in the history of the borough.

The station was packed with people and as the train entered there were loud-reports of fog signals, which had been placed on the rails. The players, on leaving the station and entering St George's-square, were received with thunderous cheers from nearly 30,000 persons who had assembled, and they were carried shoulder-high to the George Hotel, where they were entertained at dinner. After dinner the players made a tour of the town in an illuminated tramcar. The population turned out en masse to witness the scene, nearly a hundred thousand people lining the streets.

The Observer, 28 November 1909

International events also brought people into the Square. In 2012 the Olympic flame was carried through the Square and along John William Street – Robert Morris passed the torch to Rebecca Kane outside the George Hotel. And although not part of the route for the Tour de France in 2014, large screens were placed in the Square for those who wanted to watch the race as well as enjoying the temporary French market.

Cycling has a long association with St George's Square. The first 'amalgamated' run of the Huddersfield and District Amateur Cycling Association (ADACA) took place on the evening of 8 July 1891 with what could only be described as a 'procession', including a tandem and three tricycles, passing through the Square on its way to Mirfield.

> ...Owing to the way in which the spectators encroached on to the road, leaving only about one yard of it unoccupied, several spills took place upon the initial stage of the journey, but these mishaps only added to the amusement of the victims and spectators alike.
>
> *Huddersfield Daily Examiner,* 9 July 1891

Richard Hobson has been researching the history of cycling in Huddersfield and has found that at the beginning of the 1890s cycling events could always attract large numbers of spectators. Around 50 cyclists affiliated to the ADACA assembled in St George's Square on Sunday afternoon, 16 August 1891, before setting off for a Church Parade at New Mill. The vicar, the Reverend B. J. Holmes, critical of those who said that cycling on a Sunday

was a sin and himself a cyclist, had written an anthem specially for the occasion. In the following year 70 cyclists gathered in the Square before the ride to New Mill; the *Cycling* magazine declared the event 'to be a great success, the attendance being far in advance of last year'. At the time Sunday was the only day many people had to pursue leisure activities, so it was no wonder that Sunday cycling became popular – in 1894 the 'Huddersfield cycling season' opened on Palm Sunday with Ilkley as the destination before returning to Huddersfield. But in the 21st century, Katie remembers meeting in the Square for a very different type of cycling event: 'a mass cycle protest' although the destination was, once again, New Mill.

MUSIC
AND DANCE

PERHAPS THE *Huddersfield Chronicle* could have been a bit more charitable in reporting on the 'monster' gathering of non-conformist Sunday schools which took place in St George's Square on Whit Monday 1860, when it suggested

THE CHAPEL SCHOOLS
THE MONSTER GATHERING IN
ST GEORGE'S SQUARE

...By half past two, the large space of ground enclosed by the handsome edifices for which St George's Square is celebrated, was covered with a living multitude; while in each window for almost every available spot from whence a good view could be obtained, appeared crowds of fair spectators. And now the six bands of music whose performance on this grand occasion had been looked forward to with such interest, take their places in the centre of the raised platform, and the conductor Mr A. Dean, jun., ... mounts the raised dais, and is presented with the white baton of authority. A cheer greets him on his appearance; and then at a given signal, the bands strike up the fine old tune of 'Grosvenor,' and from 120 musical instruments proceed the strains of sacred harmony. This gives place to the softer and more melodious voices of the children, who, in words appropriate to the occasion, utter praises and thanksgiving. The effect is by no means so grand as the visitors anticipate, and though pleasing, has nothing in it of special attractiveness. [Hymns and extracts from oratorios played by the bands were listed]. After two hours had been thus occupied the bands struck up "God save the Queen," which was joined in by the children; and an enthusiastic cheer having been raised in honour of her Majesty, and a similar acknowledgement accorded to Mr. Dean, the children separated in the order in which they arrived, and the vast crowd, which numbered little less than 25,000 disappeared...

The singing, as before remarked, did not come up to the expectations of those assembled to listen to it, enhanced as these expectations doubtless were by the grand effect produced at the assembly above alluded to on the occasion of the peace rejoicings...

Huddersfield Chronicle, 2 June 1860.

that the children's singing might not have lived up to the expectations of spectators who had been present at the celebration to mark the end of the Crimean War. However, the article did point out that the children were damp and 'uncomfortable' from standing in the rain for two hours. Accompanying the children were the Lindley Band, Jackson's Rifle Corps Band, Huddersfield Old Band and 'amateur instrumentalists'.

Music has always played its part in the life of the Square. In addition to big religious gatherings, political demonstrations were often accompanied by several bands. Bands from the villages around the district regularly performed in the Square, sometimes announcing their programme in advance. Locally raised volunteer regiments had their own bands, and military bands from the regular army would often play there when passing through the town. But over the years many very different musical events have taken place in the Square. Both its pubs have hosted live music nights for many years.

In 1999 I was asked to work with Kirklees Council on a drug awareness and safer night clubbing event called St George's 99. We had a big stage and advertised many local acts.

PAT FULGONI, June 2022

ST. GEORGE'S '99
Live music and dance festival
FREE concert in support of the Boiling point Preventer project
**4 - 10pm
Sat 11 September 1999**
St George's Square, Huddersfield
Featuring top bands and DJs
**Kava Kava Huggy
The Bluefoot Project
Nine Invisibles
Lubby Nugget Hipstream
Yak Boy (DJ Peter Tascam)
+ special guests**
Loads of compilation CDs to give away!

In the 1980s–90s modern jazz bands played at the Head of Steam, with mainly traditional jazz (Cherry Tree Jazz Band) on Sundays at the Station Tavern (now the King's Head). My band, Swing of Things, played at the Station Tavern for a few months in the early 1990s, but we didn't bring enough of an extra crowd, so the landlord told us to go! The same pub used to regularly put on rock 'n' roll and rockabilly bands for a good few years.

STAN SAGAN, March 2022

Perhaps the most unusual musical event to take place in the Square was Barry Russell's opera, *Snogging Harold Wilson*, in November 2004. The performance, part of that year's Huddersfield Contemporary Music Festival, went ahead in the Square as planned despite the driving snow. But at least it wasn't snowing for Huddersfield Youth Opera when they performed Rimsky Korsakov's short opera *Mozart and Salieri* in the Square in July 2011.

And while there's been music in the Square, there has also been dance. Who remembers the 'Big Tap Dance' for Children in Need, which took place outside the station in November 2014, led by BBC Radio Leeds presenter Liz Green? And Huddersfield was one of just four Yorkshire towns to feature in the BBC Two Series, *Our Dancing Town* with a one-off dance through the town celebrating its history and culture, presented by dancer and choreographer Steve Elias. Huddersfield Local History Society chair Cyril Pearce appeared briefly in the programme to provide an overview of the district's history. He later commented: 'Huddersfield looked great on screen – an extended promotional video with wonderful architecture – and the dancing was pretty good too!'

Music and dance were brought together on 16 July 2023 when it has been estimated that 15,000 people gathered into St George's Square for the grand finale of HERD, a musical and artistic extravaganza featuring Kirklees-based performers and 23 'singing sheep'.

White Rose Morris in front of the station celebrating their 60th anniversary in 2013, courtesy White Rose Morris.

No-one knew what was coming next – and no-one cared. The HERD Finale in St George's Square on Sunday evening was a marvellous musical mash-up. Around 350 singers, musicians and performers put on a show in all corners of the Square and the audience – young, old or canine – just went with the flow. All HERD's 23 baaa-rmy but brilliant sheep met up in the Square and the musical event happened all around them...Passengers emerging from the train station must have thought they'd stepped off the wrong platform into a weird world where rap met brass, bhangra blended with choral and gospel sent spirits soaring as only gospel can.

MARTIN SHAW, editor, Huddersfield Hub, July 2023

Organised as part of the Kirklees Year of Music and produced by Artichoke, HERD celebrated not only the part played by the textile industry, and of course sheep, in the district's history but also its rich and varied musical traditions, some brought here by those who came to work in the mills. Over six days, the musical sheep sculptures came from all directions to finally gather in St George's Square. With names derived from the old sheep-counting song, 'Yan Tan Tethera', no two sheep were the same and each had its unique soundscape. Punk sheep, Jaggit, certainly stood out in the crowd!

At first it looked as though the hour-long finale would be blighted by rain but after just a few minutes the skies cleared. Amongst those taking part were Thabo Mkwananzi, Ruby Wood, Martin Chung, the Skelmanthorpe and Hade Edge brass band, Huddersfield Choral Society, Huddersfield Community Gospel Choir, Shepley Singers, the Bolyaan Group and Supriya Nagarajan. Children from Whitechapel C of E Primary, Headlands Junior and Newsome Junior schools performed 'Sheep Herding' and 'Yan Tan Tethera'. The concert ended on an optimistic note with a rousing rendition of 'The future is in our hands'. HERD was devised by Orlando Gough and the singing sheep were created by Huddersfield-based artist Dave Griffin. Judging by the number of cameras and phones held high, this is possibly the most photographed event ever to have taken place in the Square.

*HERD – 'Singing Sheep',
courtesy Christine Verguson.*

HERD – 'Finale'. Images courtesy of Christopher R. Marsden.

HERD – 'Finale'. Images courtesy of Janette Martin and Christine Verguson.

TRAMS AND
TROLLEY BUSES

IN JULY 1883, only six months after trams first appeared in Huddersfield, a tragic accident occurred in which seven people died and 28 were injured. The Lindley tramcar appeared to get out of control in Trinity Street. The *Huddersfield Chronicle* (6 July 1883) reported that 'the females shrieked, and, indeed, several of the male passengers did the same, and, in view of the great danger before them, it was no wonder if many lost their presence of mind.' The tramcar left the rails as it turned into Railway Street from Westgate to enter the Square and turned over onto its side. Bystanders pulled the tramcar into an upright position taking it into the Square where 'it was surrounded

Steam tram in Square, courtesy Kirklees Local Studies Library.

by a large crowd of people, all anxious for an explanation of the broken glass and damaged side'. After the Lindley Brass Band went ahead with a pre-advertised performance in St George's Square on the following evening, bandmaster Joe Kaye wrote to the *Chronicle* explaining that the bandsmen had been unaware of the seriousness of the injuries when the concert began.

Although other towns had earlier tramways, these were privately operated. Huddersfield trams were owned and run by the Corporation from their introduction in January 1883, with most services running through St George's Square. Except for the Moldgreen service, which initially used horse trams, the Huddersfield trams were hauled by steam engines. The history of Huddersfield trams and trolley buses has been particularly well documented by Roy Brook, Geoff Lumb and others. Included here are just some of the incidents that took place in the Square. What is clear, though, from W. H. Dean's testimony in 1883 is that the tram had quickly become a well-used form of transport – the Lindley tram was crowded, and travelling by tram into town had already become part of Dean's routine.

THE DREADFUL TRAMCAR ACCIDENT AT HUDDERSFIELD

Mr W. H. Dean, of Lindley, chemist, who was injured and is now at home suffering from his injuries, states that it was his usual custom to travel by the half-past-one tram to Huddersfield, but on Tuesday he was busy and only had time to catch the half-past two, and he got on the top and sat next to Mr Rowland Hall, Mr Wimpenny, and others. The car was, he states, laden to excess, persons riding on the steps and standing on the end platform at the bottom. He had little luggage with him, and when the conductor came to collect fares on the second stage, he (Mr Dean) complained about the number of people, and asked, 'What are you squeezing us like this for?' Upon that the conductor swore, and told him to mind his own business…The car had then begun to increase its speed, which was being accelerated every few yards, and when it got opposite the Mayor's warehouse, the people on the top began to make efforts to leave the car, and some jumped off near the Crown. He could not get off the car, though he tried to do so, and it was whilst he was endeavouring to do this, and to save a woman who was emerging from the car, that he was thrown down to the ground, and received severe injuries, from which he is now confined to his bed. He is being attended by Dr Porritt, and today at noon he was doing fairly. Mr Dean, by way of addendum, said the conductor made the observation to him that everyone wanted to ride, and he had hard work to keep them off.

Leeds Mercury, 5 July 1883

Steam trams waiting in John William Street, courtesy Kirklees Image Archive.

Postcard showing electric tram crossing the Square and waiting charabancs, courtesy Christine Verguson.

Accidents involving trams were not infrequent although they did not usually result in fatalities. In 1901 the Lindley tram, just three days after electric trams were first introduced on the route, in taking the bend from Westgate into the Square, went off the rails. Most passengers managed to get off before this happened but Mrs Gledhill, who had been in the Lindley tramcar when it overturned in 1883 in taking the same bend, was 'so alarmed that she fainted'. And it was not uncommon for passengers to fall as they came down the tramcar stairs – Nathan Davison had to be taken to the Infirmary when he fell when alighting in St George's Square but was then able to walk home.

The trams shared the Square with other forms of transport as well as horses and pedestrians and there were increasing concerns about safety. Alderman Glendinning expressed his fears to the Tramways committee in 1893: 'It had occurred to him that the St George's-square crossing was rather dangerous for women and children. He thought the erection of a lamp or an island would afford some safety'.

FELL ACROSS THE TRAM LINE
HUDDERSFIELD WOMAN'S NARROW ESCAPE

Today, Kate Haigh, 50 years of age who resides at the White Horse Inn, Deighton, near Huddersfield was walking across the tram line in St George's Square, Huddersfield, when she fell. The driver of an approaching car managed to pull up before the wheels reached her, but when taken from underneath the car it was found that she was in an unconscious state. She was conveyed to the Huddersfield Infirmary, and this afternoon was said to be rather better. She is suffering from very severe shock.

Yorkshire Evening Post, 23 October 1902

Trolley bus crossing diagonally across the Square, courtesy Kirklees Image Archive.

Changing the points, courtesy Kirklees Local Studies Library.

Tramway Inspector Jimmy Armitage, 39, was in the Square altering the points of a stationary tram in June 1913 when a motor-wagon coming from Viaduct Street turned sharply to the left, knocking him down. Armitage died later in the Infirmary. The conductor, who had also been injured, told the inquest that before he got off the tram car he had checked that the road was clear but did not see the approaching wagon. The wagon driver stated that at the top of Northumberland Street he had seen a tram going forward and intended to pass on the offside but, as he got nearer, he saw that the tramcar was across the rails. Seeing the two men then getting off the tramcar it was too late to avoid them. Returning a verdict of accidental death, the jury recommended that a policeman be placed at the top of Northumberland Street because the traffic there was frequently congested.

From 1933 Huddersfield's trams were gradually replaced by trolley buses and Huddersfield's last tramcar made its final journey on 29 June 1940.

Many Huddersfield children have never seen a tramcar in our streets. Ten years ago, on the 28th June, 1940, the last two tramcars arrived at the top of Northumberland Street from Brighouse and discharged their passengers. The Dunkirk evacuation had taken place only a few weeks before and the black-out regulations were strictly enforced. Consequently, we last tram passengers had our ride inside a vehicle with deep-blue tinted electric-light bulbs. At the end of the run souvenir hunters were busy. I recall two flitting away into the darkness of St. George's Square with the bamboo trolley-pole...

W. B. Stocks, *Huddersfield Daily Examiner*, 28 June 1950

An island was created in the Square for trolley buses which were often parked diagonally. One Corporation trolley bus was put to use as a call to arms in April 1939, a 'tattoo', organised by Huddersfield Territorials as part of the National Service Campaign.

> The military band and the drums and bugles of the 43rd (5th Duke of Wellington's) Anti-Aircraft Battalion, Royal Engineers, together with eight waggons (two with searchlights) paraded in front of the railway station entrance. Owing to the traffic there was little room for any large display. In the centre of the square a trolley 'bus with National Service placards was brightly illuminated. A crowd of about 5,000 people watched the short ceremony.
>
> *Yorkshire Observer*, 26 April 1939

By 1951 Huddersfield Corporation had a fleet of 140 trolley buses but in July 1968 the last of these was taken out of service. Corporation motor buses – originally a joint operation with the railway companies – had been passing through the Square from 1920 and today some bus services still run through the Square.

> I was brought up in Meltham. If I arrived at Huddersfield station after the last Hanson's bus (11pm from the bus station) I would hurry out of the station across St George's Square to catch the trolley bus to Crosland Moor – last bus 11.55pm, then walk the rest. The line-up of trolley buses at 11.55 was an impressive memory.
>
> JOHN SHEPPARD, September 2021

The National Service recruitment trolley bus, 1939, courtesy Kirklees Local Studies Library– a tram is parked alongside.

ANIMALS
IN THE SQUARE

On Monday forenoon, a wedding party from Golcar, consisting of three white-waistcoated young men and three maidens, preceded by an "old father," who was to give away the bride at church, entered the town of Huddersfield, walking peaceably, but with their faces suffused with blushes, along the causeways. What caused them to blush, and the immediate collection of an immense crowd of spectators, which accompanied them to the gates of the parish church was an extraordinary procession of twelve donkeys (each mounted by a young man) which attended the wedding party as a guard of honour. The donkeys and their riders were gracefully decorated with garlands of straw and dirty rags, and the riders carried broomsticks on their shoulders, a la drawn swords. As this extraordinary cavalcade proceeded along the streets, the crowd continued rapidly to increase, until the streets became entirely blocked, and it was with considerable difficulty that the police could clear a passage for the bridal party to the church. The chief constable and the police soon learnt that the donkeys and their riders were obnoxious to the wedding folks, and by their desire the donkeys, who were standing at the gates of the church were ordered to "move on"... The "silken knot of matrimony" having at length been tied, the wedding party was seen to emerge from the back door of the church, and wend its way through the back-yard gates into Saint Peter's-street, and from thence through St George's square to the railway station, about 100 yards above. The information was soon given to the donkeys and the crowd, who immediately set off pell-mell up Kirkgate and John William-street, to the station. The scene here baffled description. Let the reader imagine a crowd of several thousands, and such a donkey procession as we have described, hastening under such circumstances to catch the wedding party, and about half-a-dozen policemen vainly endeavouring to arrest their progress. It was all the most lively imagination can picture. Stalls, fruit tables and old women being knocked over. The wedding folks, however, got safely ensconced in the London and North western booking-office, and the doors locked against the donkeys and the crowd, but there was no train to Golcar for nearly two hours. The donkeys were driven away by the police, the crowd soon afterwards dispersed, and the wedding party left in a cab, and proceeded to Golcar.

Morning Advertiser, 9 August 1853

WE WILL NEVER know why the donkey procession chased the wedding party from the parish church and across St George's Square to the station, but animals have always played a part in the Square's story. Imagine the sounds and the smells of the Square when most of the traffic was horse-drawn – runaway horses were not unknown although not everyone will have had the experience of one correspondent to the *Huddersfield Chronicle*.

A DANGEROUS PRACTICE

...I refer to the practice of taking horses out of cabs in the public street and putting others in. On Monday last about 2pm, I was going along John William-street to the station, and in turning the corner to cross St George's-square, I saw a man taking a horse out of a cab, and another one standing with its heels in a good position to command any one crossing to and from the station. I had no sooner began to cross than this brute up with her heels, caught me on the side and left arm and sent me reeling back. She then launched out again with both heels, and screaked in such a way as to convince those who saw and heard that the animal is a most dangerous one ought not to be left in a public throughfare. Fortunately for me, the first blow, together with my own effort, carried me away just in time out of reach of the horse's heels, which were thrown into the air time after time, and in such a way to convince me she had had much practice...Hoping that the authorities will see such a dangerous practice is put a stop to.- I enclose my card, and remain, yours very truly,

NO ENEMY TO CABBY,
Commercial-street, Feb. 6th, 1866

Huddersfield Chronicle, 17 February 1866.

Perhaps the most curious procession of animals in the Square took place during the First World War when a collection was being made in support of the Mayoress's fund for sick and disabled horses.

... Chief interest, of course, centred on the procession which was formed in St George's Square. The variety of entrants was remarkable in many respects. There were tradesmen's turnouts, railway vans, and private carriages, ladies and gentlemen on horseback, and all kinds of dumb animals. Perhaps the most interesting of all was the zebra from the Halifax Zoo, which was lent by Mr S Hinds, the head keeper. Then there were two smart Shetland ponies which came in for much admiration...

Huddersfield Daily Examiner, 26 July 1915

Today we are much more likely to see dogs in the Square as they accompany their owners to the station, to an event in the Square or even to find refreshment 'When It All Gets Too Much' as Dan Reilly's image, specially commended in our photo competition, Capturing St George's Square, illustrates! And where would the St Patrick's Day Parade be without the Austonley Wolfhounds?

'When It All Gets Too Much' by Dan Reilly – specially commended in the Capturing St George's Square 2020-2022 photo competition.

Take a close look at the buildings around the Square and see how many animals you can spot - you may even find a dragon!

The Austonley Irish Wolfhounds, courtesy Huddersfield St Patrick's Day Parade

My grandma Peggy Mackay used to tell me that her Dad, Arthur Holt, used to tell her that when the clock struck 12, the lion on Lion Chambers would climb down and walk around St George's Square. She then told me that the clock never actually struck.

CATRIONA SWINDELLS, September 2021

But the lion did 'climb down' from its pedestal – in 1977 when, after more than a century of presiding over the Square, it was taken down to be replaced by a fibre-glass copy.

The lion in chains? Awaiting demolition in 1977 -
photograph taken by the late Brian Worsnop, WRNS Pictures.

CELEBRATION OF THE "GUNPOWDER PLOT."

– The famous plot, which, as every one should know, was intended to have blown up King James the First, and which was discovered on the 5th. November, was celebrated at Huddersfield by what might be termed a pyrotechnic display in St George's-square. The police authorities, whose experiences and recollections of similar rejoicings in previous years are not of the most pleasant kind, conceded a licence to, and resolved not to interfere with, those who might be disposed to indulge in a little merry-making. Consistent with the convenience and safety of the public, this was a prudent course to adopt; and the youthful "Guido Faux" were not backward in appreciating and making good use of the liberty thus granted. Hundreds of persons, - old and young, male and female,- wended their way to the square, which presented a scene of extraordinary confusion, equalled only by a charge on the battle field, or an attack upon a fortress. The discharge of firearms was loud and incessant; rockets pierced the air in rapid succession; and at intervals the square was brilliantly illuminated. Every conceivable description of fireworks was bought up, and the vendors were all the evening actively engaged in clearing out their stocks. Crowds assembled to witness the fete; and it is certainly an astonishing fact that not a single mishap is known to have occurred.

Huddersfield Chronicle, 11 November 1865

FROM FIREWORKS TO FESTIVALS

Huddersfield Food and Drink Festival 2001 with chef Barrington Douglas, and David Wyles holding the microphone, courtesy David Wyles.

THE POLICE AUTHORITIES would certainly have been pleased that Guy Fawkes night in 1865 passed off without incident; the previous year's celebrations ended with smashed windows at the George and at Shaw's warehouse. But, over the years, firework displays have accompanied many of the big events held in the Square, usually in a more organised fashion.

There were fireworks in St George's Square at the gala launch of the International Markets Festival in July 1999 which brought 7000 people into the Square and traders from 11 countries to the town. An appreciation of local tradition and international influences is reflected in many of the festivals in the Square. The first Huddersfield Food and Drink Festival put on by the Town Centre Association took place in August 2001. Organised by Huddersfield Town Centre Manager, David Wyles, it became an annual event but was cancelled in 2020 due to COVID. The Food and Drink Festival was to make a welcome return in 2023, but in Greenhead Park. However torrential rain meant that the Festival had to be cancelled.

I organised the first Food and Drink Festival in August 2001, which grew from strength to strength over the following years. The first years were a little chaotic with such events as pizza tossing in which the mayor of Kirklees at the time, Cllr Margaret Hall, gamely participated. Unfortunately, my attempt at tossing the uncooked, flour covered pizza was a little ambitious. It narrowly missed the Mayor and hit her attendant. My career survived and I had many enjoyable incidents at the festival, especially in the demonstration theatre, with cook-offs between BBC Look North presenters, football and rugby league players and some of the area's best chefs.

DAVID WYLES December 2021

Katie remembers 'an Xmas night out at the Hygge tent'. The Huddersfield Winter Festival, organised by Huddersfield Live, has brightened up December in the town since 2017 – only taking a year off because of COVID in 2020 - and a central feature of the festival is a large tipi in St George's Square which provides a venue for performances throughout the Festival.

In 2014 the Square had a distinctly French feel, which some remember better than the event it was designed to celebrate. The French rural scene had appeared overnight in St George's Square complete with animals, fruit,

> The French farm display! Who could forget that outstanding set up with live animals and real French farmers. Cannot recall why it came but it was tremendous nonetheless.
>
> ADRIAN LEE March 2022

> In July 2014 when there was a temporary fruit, vegetable and flower market in St George's Square as part of the celebrations surrounding Tour de France coming to Yorkshire. During the race itself large screens were placed in the square and many people watched the race outdoors. Inspired by Tour de France we cycled along the narrow canal to Slaithwaite that day!
>
> JANETTE MARTIN August 2021

Sunflowers at the (Tour de France) French Market 2014, courtesy John Lambe.

Janette and Maria with a stallholder at the French Market 2014, courtesy Janette Martin.

flowers and vegetable plots tended by actual French gardeners. It was a surprise pop up event to celebrate the Tour de France's Grand Départ from Yorkshire.

Another event which has utilised the Square to great effect in recent decades has been the Festival of Light. The grandeur of the buildings has been used to dramatic effect whilst the space has provided a perfect stage for fantastic light creations and firework finales.

Festival of Light finale in the Square 2007, courtesy Alan Stopher.

For many years the Festival of Light was a spectacular winter event bringing street artists from all over Europe. Each one culminated in a firework display, itself a link to a local business. Huddersfield Railway Station is lit up by strange lanterns with fireworks as a backdrop.

ALAN STOPHER May 2023

Huddersfield's fantastic Festival of Light ran for several years and I'm pretty sure I went along on more than one occasion. In 2007 the procession, which featured giant sea creatures, started at St Peter's Gardens and ended with fireworks in St George's Square. The procession was created and staged by Plasticiens Volants from France

CHRISTINE VERGUSON August 2021

Following the Covid pandemic, the town's annual St Patrick's Day Parade has taken place here – in 2022 Huddersfield could take pride in organising the 'second shortest St Patrick's Day Parade in the world'! Starting at the station steps it was all of 32 metres long, the same number as there are counties in Ireland. And the Huddersfield Carnival's welcome return in 2023 was preceded by a Carnival Performance alongside the St Patrick Day's Parade.

St Patrick Day Parade, 12 March 2023, courtesy Flaming Creations.

Huddersfield Carnival's welcome return in 2023 was preceded by a Carnival performance during the St Patrick's Day Parade, courtesy Flaming Creations.

In June 2023 Kirklees Pride brought music, comedy and much more to the Square in a celebration of Huddersfield's LGBTQ+ community. And the Square has also played host to Big Screen Weekends. From Lion Buildings to Pride Rock...

> I have a cherished memory of sitting in deck chairs with my very excited children to watch the film of the Lion King on a big screen in St George's Square underneath the plaster lion on the Lion Buildings
>
> REBECCA GILL March 2023

POETICAL EPISTLE

I take him the crumbs outside
And he looks as much as to say
You're a very good boy to bring me these;
I'll pay you back some day!

Dear Androcles, the lion too
Has his place of high renown,
He looks as well as anything
That decorates the town.

He's stood the test of many a storm,
But you know he cannot feel,
He's like his friend across the Square,
The honoured Sir Robert Peel.

Dear sir, I came from Huddersfield,
About seven months ago,
And now I live in Dewsbury,
I thought you'd like to know.

C. W. POGSON

Children's Column, Supplement to
Dewsbury Reporter, 29 March 1884

INSPIRED
BY THE SQUARE

POGSON'S POEM, WRITTEN for children in 1884, may well have been the first poem to feature the town's most famous lion but it is certainly not the last. It makes an appearance in Simon Armitage's poem *Leo* in his collection, *CloudCuckooLand*, published in 1997. But look carefully at Huddersfield's stone buildings and you will find many more – staying in the Square there are at least 20 on Estate Buildings alone.

Architectural historian Chris Marsden has, for a number of years, been hunting Huddersfield's many lions and has led several 'lion hunt' guided walks around the town centre. In 2022, as part of Historic England's High Streets Heritage Action Zone cultural programme, together with photographer Laura Mateescu, he devised the wonderfully titled Joy of a Roar project. Over 100 people took part, not only making paper lion masks in a series of workshops but modelling them in studio shoots. All 40 portraits were then put on display turning Station Street and other nearby places into a street art gallery, celebrating health and wellbeing through sport, play and dance.

Devised by Chris Marsden and Laura Mateescu, The Joy of a Roar turned Station Street into a temporary art gallery. Photo, courtesy Christine Verguson.

Noël Woodward Spencer (1900-1986) was head of the Huddersfield Technical College from 1934 to 1946 and, while in Huddersfield, he sketched many of the town's buildings, publishing them in two volumes of 'Scrap' books. Writing in the Foreword to the first book, Spencer remarked that, 'we must confess that Huddersfield cannot be called a beautiful town'. That said, he believed that it 'contained much of interest to the artist'. The drawings Spencer made for these books are held by Huddersfield Art Gallery and were published in one volume in 1990 to mark the 50th anniversary of the building's completion. Spencer's drawing of Lion Buildings captures a scene from the 1940s with people waiting to catch a trolley bus.

Lion Buildings

Noël Spencer's drawing of Lion Buildings from A Scrap Book of Huddersfield, 1945 © Estate of Noel Spencer

Huddersfield Station - a nocturnal view, photographed by David Wimpenny.

In the 1990s, inspired by walking through the Square in the winter months after it had been raining, David Wimpenny's photograph, included here, is a study in light, capturing the station as it appeared just after midnight. And David has also told us of the ingenuity that was required in the dark room to reflect the clusters of light around the lamps.

On numerous occasions I had seen the effect of the sheen on the street and in the pavements on the Yorkshire stone. It's just the reflections. It was a Sunday night. We went down there intentionally to take these photos from the left and the right-hand side so to cut down movement causing blur on the picture, I positioned myself under the canopy of the George Hotel to avoid any rain in the lens and took a series of shots...I had to go down a few weeks before and see when it got the quietest...

DAVID WIMPENNY March 2023

Huddersfield.
*Harold Wilson.

Today the Square, the station, not to mention Harold, provide inspiration for Huddersfield Urban Sketch Meet, a group led by artist Jo Blaker. Huddersfield Urban Sketch Meets happen monthly, are free and open to all.

Sketches by Jane Horton.

Urban Sketching is an international movement where people draw from observation, as opposed to secondary sources, to record a particular place at a particular time. St George's Square has been our subject matter on more than one occasion as Harold is the meeting point for our group - Huddersfield Urban Sketch Meets. The buildings around the square offer a variety of architectural details and structures. The people, cars, trees, even pigeons all add interest and make this location a fun place to draw throughout the year.

JO BLAKER July 2023

In 2021 the start of the biennial WOVEN in Kirklees festival, curated by Natalie Walton, was launched by the installation of a huge yard bomb at the front of the station with other squares from the Big Rainbow Knitters decorating other part of the Square.

The WOVEN in Kirklees festival is a celebration of all things textiles from Kirklees textile heritage, its current industry and innovation and its creativity. in 2021 the festival supported the knitting community to yarn bomb Huddersfield train station with the most wonderful rainbow. This was in response to COVID lockdown offering people the opportunity to meet online and work together even if they could not be together. The team of knitters felt no installation would be complete without a scarf and mask for Harold Wilson.

NATALIE WALTON August 2023

Yarn bombing 2021 - Harold Wilson in a face mask!
Courtesy, WOVEN in Kirklees

At THE WHITE LINE Celebration, 21 August 2022 - Photos by Laura Mateescu, courtesy of Let's Go Yorkshire.

On 22 August 2022 the Square was filled with music, dance, theatre and film as THE WHITE LINE Celebration marked the 75th anniversary of the Partition of British India, curated by Mandeep Samra of Let's Go Yorkshire. The afternoon included a performance of a new play from Chol Theatre, *Three Pounds in My Pocket*, based on the experiences of people who came to Huddersfield from the Indian sub-continent in the 1960s.

St George's Square has over the years been a space for some of the town's biggest events, but it also provided the location for some very personal moments. Jessica has been kind enough to share her story.

Me and my fiancé got engaged at St. George's Square on the 14th August 2020. We had been to Gringo's for a meal...and afterwards he led me to St. George's Square where we sat on one of the benches. It was during one of the breaks of Covid lockdown so it was still very quiet. He then passed me a piece of paper. When I opened it, it said 'Will you marry me?' and as I turned to him he opened the box with the ring in it. St. George's Square is such a lovely space with so much history and beautiful architecture. It really was a lovely spot for a lockdown engagement

JESSICA October 2021

Postcards, courtesy Christine Verguson.

CONCLUSION

THIS BOOK MARKS the end of Huddersfield Local History Society's Memories of Our Square project. While we have used the traditional tools of the historian – archival research and gathering testimony - to put this work together, by taking part in Huddersfield's High Streets Heritage Action Zone cultural programme we have also been able to reflect some of the amazing creative activity which continues to thrive across the district and is very much part of our story.

Although St George's Square was built originally as a private venture by the Ramsden family, from its very beginning the town has made the Square its own in so many ways. It has provided the backdrop for performance, protest and celebration in ways the Ramsdens could not have envisaged. Yet, except for the time part of it was given over to gardens, missed by many, and Sir Robert Peel's eventual replacement by Lord Wilson, the Square's appearance has not changed a great deal since the completion of Estate Buildings in 1871. The cabs are still there although no longer drawn by horses.

Estate Buildings is now being converted into housing, aimed at bringing people back into the town centre, and the George is being refurbished as a hotel which it is hoped will be more suited to today's needs. From the men and women who crowded into the Square demanding the right to vote to the rousing rendition of 'The future is in our hands' at the HERD finale in July 2023, it has also been a place where many have gathered to look forward.

In the meantime, people go to and from the station and traffic passes through the Square, which still provides a place where people can come to meet under the watchful eyes of Harold Wilson. The newsboys, trams and trolley buses have disappeared but it is certain that new stories will continue to be written in the long history of Huddersfield's St George's Square.

TIMELINE

1840s

1846
Earl Fitzwilliam laid the foundation stone of the Railway Station [9 October].

1847
Railway from Huddersfield to Cooper Bridge opened [2 August].

1849
William Wallen began staking out the ground for the new George Hotel [31 January].

Railway from Huddersfield to Manchester opened [13 July].

1850s

1850
Railway from Huddersfield to Penistone and Holmfirth Branch opened [1 July].

1851
George Hotel opened [22 September].

1853
A Coade stone lion weighing 7 tons was placed on top of Samuel Oldfield's Royal Arcade, the name of which was changed to the Lion Arcade.

1854
John William Street extension of the George Hotel built.

Lion Arcade, designed by J.P. Pritchett, opened [23 January].

1856
Tite's Building completed, originally used as warehouses and offices by woollen manufacturers.

1858
A pair of Russian cannon from Sebastapol given to the town and placed on the station forecourt.

1859
Britannia Buildings completed, designed by William Cocking for George Crosland & Sons, woollen manufacturers and merchants as warehouse, offices and showroom.

1860s

1865
An estimated 18,000 people crammed into the Square to take part in the election hustings [July].

1866
Thousands of working men and a dozen bands crammed into the Square in support of the Parliamentary Reform Bill which would extend the franchise.

1868
Work began on the site of the Ramsden Estate Buildings with the demolition of the old Cherry Tree Hotel.

1870s

1870
Ramsden Estate Buildings opened [September].

1873
Unveiling of statue of Sir Robert Peel by Lord Houghton attracted huge crowds, estimated at 40,000 people [3 June].

1874
Laundry and kitchen extension, designed by W.H. Crossland, added to the George Hotel.

1878
Cannon removed to Longley Hall. In 1942, they were salvaged for the war effort.

1880s

1884
Demonstration led by Liberal MPs in support of electoral reforms. Described as the biggest and most important political gathering held in the town up to that time.

1890s

1895
Northern Rugby Football Union established at a meeting at the George Hotel [29 August].

1899
George Hotel further extended.

1900s

1902
Britannia Buildings, Huddersfield Building Society leased offices to rear of ground floor.

1908
Britannia Buildings became Head Office of Huddersfield Building Society.

Emmeline Pankhurst led a "Votes for Women" demonstration organised by her daughter Adela, with five speaker platforms arranged around the Peel statue.

The square was reportedly full with estimates of between 20,000 to 50,000 in the crowd [27 September].

1910s

1914
Large numbers gathered to greet the arrival of Belgian refugees at the Railway Station.

1916
J. B. Flanders burnt his call-up papers [May].

1918
Armistice Day [November].

1919
First of attempt to convert the Lion Arcade into a cinema.

1920s

1920
With the purchase of the Ramsden Estate, the Estate Buildings and George Hotel became the property of Huddersfield Corporation.

1922
Huddersfield Town returned with the FA Cup, greeted by a crowd estimated at between 25,000 and 30,000.

Plans to convert Lion Arcade into a cinema were approved but the scheme seems to have been dropped shortly afterwards.

1924
Britannia Buildings sold to Huddersfield Building Society for £24,000.

1926
Internal alterations to Britannia Buildings made and a new façade added in Art Deco style by Clifford Hickson.

1940s

1940
Last two Huddersfield tramcars ended their journey at the top of Northumberland Street [28 June].

1945
Winston Churchill addressed crowd during general election campaign [27 June].

1949
Statue of Sir Robert Peel, said to be in a disgraceful condition, removed to depot [October]. The Aberdeen granite plinth re-erected in Ravensknowle Park [March 1971].

1960s

1968
Railway Station front and Platform One bought by Huddersfield Corporation.

1970s

1977
Lion Buildings: the disintegrating lion sculpture
replaced by a fibre-glass copy.

1990s

1992
Following a £1 million programme of
regeneration and restoration, St. George's Square
recognised as an important example of Victorian civic
planning and awarded a Diploma of Merit in the Europa
Nostra Awards.

1994
Britannia Buildings. After mergers leading to the formation of the
Yorkshire Building Society, the building proves too small to use as
the headquarters of the group and is sold.

1999
Statue of Harold Wilson unveiled by Prime Minister,
Tony Blair [9 July].

2000s

2001
First Huddersfield Food and Drink Festival
took place in the Square [August].

2004
Performance of Barry Russell's opera, Snogging Harold Wilson, in
the Square in driving snow.

Revival of the town's May Day march ending in a rally in St George's
Square ahead of the European elections. Kurdish, Ethiopian and
Albanian refugees joined in.

2005
Yorkshire Building Society's Britannia Buildings office closed.

2007
The Queen visited Huddersfield University. She and the Duke of
Edinburgh were entertained by the Huddersfield Choral Society
performing from a stage in the Square before boarding the Royal
Train [24 May].

2008
Work began on the re-vamping of St George's Square [March].

2009
St George's Square re-ordered with the addition of paving, fountains
and a controversial water feature. The work involved moving the
statue of Harold Wilson. The project overran by 7 months and
cost £4 million. The original contractors went into administration.
Officially opened October.

2010s

2010

St George's Square Revival Project won RIBA White Rose Award. Design by Whitelaw Turkington Landscape Architects.

2011

Huddersfield Youth Opera performed Rimsky Korsakov's 'Mozart and Salieri' [25 July].

Libyans celebrated hope for a brighter future for their country with song, dance and fireworks [25 October].

2012

Huddersfield Town launched a new kit [12 June].

Olympic torch paraded through the Square. About 2000 people gathered in a 'Peace Protest' to campaign against a film that was considered anti-Islamic [8 October].

2013

George Hotel closed. Bought by dentist, Dr. Altaf Hussain.

White Rose Morris Men celebrated Ruby Anniversary in the Square [6 May].

Businessman Junior Rashid opened LaLa's, a restaurant with 120 covers offering Kashmiri cuisine in the marble surroundings of the former banking hall of the Yorkshire Building Society in Britannia Buildings.

2014

Tite's Buildings converted into student accommodation with 40 bedrooms in 19 units. The £1.4 million project privately funded with a grant from the Government's Clusters of Empty Homes project. Architects: Aedas.

In celebration of the Tour de France starting in Yorkshire and passing through Huddersfield, the Square was turned into a French farmyard [July].

2016

Hands off Huddersfield Royal Infirmary: rallies attracted large numbers to Square as part of campaign opposing threatened closure of A&E department in Huddersfield [23 January, 27 February].

David Lammy MP addressed an audience in support of the 'Remain' campaign on the EU Referendum [27 May].

2017

Thousands greeted the Huddersfield Town football team's open top bus and celebrated their promotion to the Premier League [May].

Huddersfield's first ever Winter Festival saw three giant tepees erected in St. George's Square [November-December].

2019
Global Climate Strike, organised by Extinction Rebellion, attracted hundreds of protesters to Square [20 September].

2020s

2020
George Hotel bought by Kirklees Council.

Crowds gathered in the Square to express solidarity with Black Lives Matter [13 June].

Rugby League Challenge Cup, Grand Final Trophy and the Men's and Wheelchair World Cup displayed in St George's Square [25 August].

2021
Historic England's Huddersfield High Streets Heritage Action Zone, a three-year programme, begins, bringing many different activities to St George's Square

Conservation Architects Bowman Riley appointed to oversee refurbishment of George Hotel.

2022
Conservation work begins on George Hotel

Work begins on the restoration of Estate Buildings

THE FUTURE?

Timeline created by Brian Haigh, May 2021

SELECT BIBLIOGRAPHY AND OTHER SOURCES

Some of the material included here has been taken from collections - including the Ramsden Estate papers - held by the West Yorkshire Archive Service, Kirklees. Extensive use has also been made of the British Newspaper Archive (www.britishnewspaperarchive.co.uk).

PUBLISHED

Armitage, Simon, *CloudCuckooLand* (London, 1997)

Brook, Roy, *The Story of Huddersfield* (London, 1968)

Brook, Roy, *Huddersfield Corporation Tramways* (Accrington, 1983)

Brook, Roy, *The Trolleybuses of Huddersfield* (Rochdale, 1976)

Chadwick, Stanley, *"All Stations to Manchester": The Centenary of the Huddersfield and Manchester Railway and Standedge Tunnel* (Huddersfield, 1949)

Chadwick, Stanley, *Railway Wonder: Development of a Town (Huddersfield, 1984)*

Clarkson, D. L., 'St George's Square and the new town of Huddersfield', *Old West Riding* 9 (Huddersfield, 1989)

Dennis, Richard, *English Industrial Cities of the Nineteenth century: A Social Geography* (Cambridge, 1984)

Earnshaw, Alan, *Scenes from the Past: 20 Railways in and around Huddersfield, Part One* (Huddersfield, 1993)

Griffiths, David, *Joseph Brook of Greenhead: 'Father of the Town'* (Huddersfield, 2013)

Haigh, Brian & Gillooley, Susan, *A Century of Huddersfield* (Stroud, 2000)

Haigh, E. A. Hilary (Ed.), *Huddersfield: A most handsome town* (Huddersfield, 1992)

Heywood, Brian (Ed.), *Huddersfield in World War 1* (Upper Calder, 2014)

Kipling, Lesley & Brooke, Alan, *Huddersfield: A History & Celebration* (Dinton, 2005)

Law, Edward, *Joseph Kaye: Builder of Huddersfield* (Huddersfield, 1989)

Liddington, Jill, *Rebel Girls: Their fight for the vote* (London, 2006)

Marsden, Christopher and Andrew Caveney, *Huddersfield in 50 Buildings* (Stroud, 2019)

Pearce, Cyril, *Comrades in Conscience: The story of an English community's opposition to the Great War* (London, 2001)

Royle, Edward (Ed.), *Power in the Land: The Ramsdens and their Huddersfield estate, 1542-1920* (Huddersfield, 2020)

Salveson, Paul, *Our Beautiful Station: Huddersfield 1847-2002* (2nd. Ed, 2001)

Samra, Mandeep Kaur, *The Boy Who Lost His Home But Carried Light* (Huddersfield, 2023)

Spencer, Noel, *A Scrap Book of Huddersfield*: Reproduced from the two original volumes in celebration of the 50th Anniversary of Huddersfield Library and Art Gallery (Huddersfield 1990, 1st. ed, 1947)

Whomsley, Denis, 'A Landed Estate and the Railway: Huddersfield 1844-1854', *The Journal of Transport History*, vol. ss-2, 4 (September 1974).

Wyles, David, *The Buildings of Huddersfield: Five architectural walks* (Huddersfield 1984, rev. ed. 2006)

UNPUBLISHED

Perks, Robert, 'Liberalism and the Challenge of Labour, 1885-1914', unpublished PhD thesis, Huddersfield Polytechnic, 1989

WEBSITES

British Newspaper Archive
https://www.britishnewspaperarchive.co.uk/

Huddersfield Exposed
https://huddersfield.exposed/wiki/Welcome

Huddersfield Local History Society
https://www.huddersfieldhistory.org.uk/

Kirklees Image Archive
https://kirkleesimages.org.uk/

Memories of Our Square
https://oursquare.huddersfieldhistory.org.uk/

Underground Histories
https://undergroundhistories.wordpress.com/

OUR SQUARE

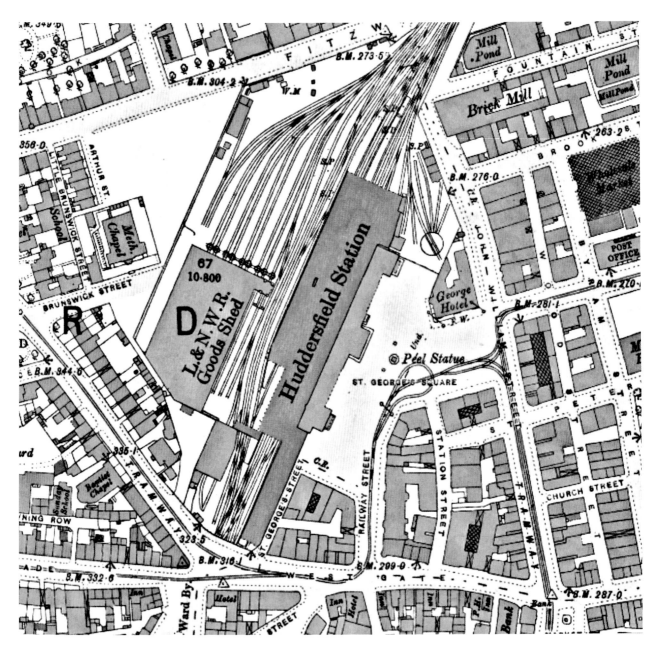

St George's Square, Huddersfield - Ordnance Survey
(surveyed 1887-1889, published 1893), CCXLVI.15